NAVIGATING THE TEENAGE YEARS

"Sue's extensive knowledge and genuine compassion for teenagers and their families shines through this wonderfully clear and helpful book – I predict it's going to be a 'must-read' for anyone who has a teenager in their lives!"

Jane Smedley, marketing consultant and parent

"Sue Saunders has done a great service to parents, teachers and psychotherapy by writing this wise, practical and inspirational book. Every growing family would benefit from it, as would school teachers, youth workers and general practitioners."

Ivan Tyrrell, FHGI, psychotherapist and co-founder of the Human Givens Approach

"This book is packed with useful insights and tips that should prove immensely useful to both the parent(s) of a teenage child, to the teenage child themselves and indeed to any person fortunate enough to get the opportunity to read this invaluable book."

Joe Griffin, BSc Hons (Psych), M.Phil (Psych) AFBPsS, FHGI and co-founder of the Human Givens Approach

"*Navigating the Teenage Years* by Human Givens psychotherapist Sue Saunders is a practical and comprehensive roadmap to navigating and negotiating your way through the many teenage trials and tribulations. Sue is an experienced and accomplished psychotherapist who has refashioned her craft using Human Givens principles, which underpin this entire text. The set of organising ideas known as the Human Givens approach to counselling and psychotherapy has gained increasing currency as a practical and balanced template, to enable people of all ages comprehend and attain their emotional needs.

This publication is suitable for a wide range of people who work with teenagers, including parents, teachers, grandparents, siblings and of course teens themselves, who will be impressed by this practical and balanced book which from start to finish is imbued with wisdom, clarity, empathy and a common-sense approach to emotional matters which can at times seem overwhelming during the teen years."

Dr Declan Lyons PhD, MSc, MRCP (UK) MRCPsych, HG Dip

"In this book Sue Saunders offers a comprehensive and comprehensible guide to living and working with teenagers. This is an insightful volume which is informed by personal experience, and by the author's professional experience as a Human Givens therapist. It is the wealth of drawn-upon personal and professional experience which ensures that the 'compassionate approach' promised by the subtitle is secured. Those who read this book will not only gain valuable understanding about what makes their teenage offspring tick, but they will also gain greater critical understanding of their own attitudes and behaviours, and of how these attitudes and behaviours may chime with or be antithetical to the needs of the teenage members of their families. The book benefits greatly from the compassionate approach of Human Givens thinking to meeting adolescent and emerging adults' needs, and readers will gain deep insight into how to communicate and interact with the teenage members of their family.

The book aspires to be a guide for parents, but its impartial, objective and insightful content means that it could be useful reading for educators working with teenagers, and for teenagers themselves who could, by reading it, gain greater understanding of the complex environment in which they have to develop and mature. The book might even help them to improve the skills necessary to communicate and negotiate with their parents."

Prof Stephen Hill, Professor of Lifelong Learning,
University of Gloucestershire

"Grounded and insightful, a really accessible parenting resource."
Jane Creaner-Glen, parent of teenagers

NAVIGATING THE TEENAGE YEARS

A Compassionate Approach

SUE SAUNDERS

ORPEN PRESS

Published by
Orpen Press Ltd

email: info@orpenpress.com
www.orpenpress.com

Paperback ISBN 978-1-909895-64-5
ePub ISBN 978-1-909895-65-2
Kindle ISBN 978-1-909895-66-9
PDF ISBN 978-1-909895-67-6

Printed in Dublin by SPRINTprint Ltd

This book is dedicated to Dave, Alan and Jamie with love

Disclaimer

This book is designed to increase knowledge, awareness and understanding of issues surrounding the psychological development of teenagers. It is not intended to replace the advice that your own doctor or therapist can give you. If you are concerned by any of the issues raised in this book make sure you consult a qualified professional. Whilst every effort has been made to ensure the accuracy of the information and material contained in this book, nevertheless it is possible that errors or omissions may occur in the content. The author and publishers assume no responsibility for and give no guarantees or warranties concerning the accuracy, completeness or up-to-date nature of the information provided in this book.

Preface

All adults were teenagers once upon a time and, as I know from my own personal and professional experience, it can be a fraught, difficult stage in life. Life seems to be getting more stressful for us all – adults, teenagers and children alike – so whatever we can do to assist parents, teachers and teenagers to move through this stage with as much support as possible can only lead to a more positive future for all of us. Teenagers are the adults of the future. It will be up to them to shape society for the future. We are their role models, and the more compassion we can bring to helping them through these years, the more we will help create a compassionate world for humanity.

The approach I have taken in this book is encapsulated in the title: *Navigating the Teenage Years: A Compassionate Approach*. I have used the framework of the Human Givens approach along with the latest neuroscientific research to assist in acquiring an understanding of the teenage brain and in developing compassion for the changes they are encountering. I have found that through using the Human Givens approach and seeing others through the lens of emotional needs, I have been better able to view both myself and others more compassionately. It has greatly enhanced my work and it allows me to assist others (both teenagers and adults) to see each other differently, increase empathy and be more understanding of each other.

When an adult sees a youngster compassionately and understands the needs they are attempting to meet, they are less likely to judge them and so can help them improve their behaviour. When a teenager sees the adult's viewpoint and how their behaviour may be driven by their anxiety for the safety of their children or students, they too can be more compassionate towards the adult population.

I hope you enjoy reading the book as much as I did writing it and my sincere thanks to all the people who have assisted me along the way.

ACKNOWLEDGEMENTS

I first came across the Human Givens approach in 2004 when I read *Human Givens: The New Approach to Emotional Heath and Clear Thinking* by Joe Griffin and Ivan Tyrrell. I had a background in psychotherapy and was greatly impressed by this practical, down-to-earth approach. It is based on sound scientific principles and shed light on many questions and anomalies I had come across in both my work and my personal life. It provided me with a framework that allowed me to make sense of myself and to understand and have compassion for others.

So, when I was approached to write a book on teenagers it was inevitable that I would approach this subject through the lens of the Human Givens approach. I would like to take this opportunity to acknowledge and thank both Joe Griffin and Ivan Tyrrell for their writings, their comprehensive training and their support over the past decade. I would also like to thank all my colleagues in the Human Givens College and Human Givens Institute who have supported me over the years and added greatly to my own development and knowledge.

My thanks also to Ailbhe O'Reilly for her belief in me and to Eileen O'Brien, Fiona Dunne and James Fox for their many helpful suggestions and refinements; their support was invaluable.

I would like to express my sincere gratitude to the many people who supported and stuck by me in writing this book, especially to my dear friend Brenda O'Hanlon, whose support through the painstaking months of writing has been unwavering; I'm not sure it would have been completed without it. My thanks also to all my colleagues and friends, Cathriona Edwards, Carol Harper, Julian Penton, Maureen Gilbert, Jane Glen and the many others who have supported me throughout this process whose names I may have failed to mention. Not forgetting my own family whose belief and support I genuinely cherish and for which I am eternally grateful.

CONTENTS

Contents

Contents

Contents

Contents

Contents

INTRODUCTION

Being an adolescent is not easy, and being the parent, guardian or any adult dealing with an adolescent can be challenging for the best of us. Almost overnight, your darling son or daughter has gone from being a sweet, adorable child to being a grumpy, sighing, sulking, moody, monosyllabic know-it-all with attitude, who thinks you are just beyond stupid – this from the child who seemed to adore you only a year ago or less.

What has happened in the intervening period is that they have crossed into the next phase of their life – adolescence – and neither your life nor theirs will ever be the same again. The goal of adolescence is independence, and as such it is a very important stage of life. During this time the young person is undergoing the changes that are necessary to prepare them for adulthood and independence. Apart from surviving these tumultuous years, your job is also to support your teenager through these changes as best you can.

However, in order to appreciate these changes some level of understanding of what is actually happening inside the teenager, in both their bodies and their brains, can really help. But you don't need to be a neuroscientist to understand what these changes are and how they affect a youngster. An overview can give you the understanding you need to help support them.

Before we begin to look at the changes that take place in the body and brain of a teenager, and why these changes cause such difficulties, it is useful to have a general overview of the human brain, and how it operates – not least because some knowledge of the brain and its functions can give us a better understanding of both our own and other people's irrational behaviour.

Part I

UNDERSTANDING OURSELVES

1

UNDERSTANDING OUR BRAIN

The brain of twenty-first-century man, woman and child has evolved from the brain of our prehistoric ancestors, which was designed to cope with, and deal with, a very different environment from the one we live in today. Over the millennia, the human brain has evolved into a three-part organ, or, to put it another way, a number of brains working together. Some sections of the brain are more primitive than others; these sections are very similar to those of our mammalian ancestors. Nature, being very economical, continues to use these sections rather than create completely new parts.

WHAT'S IN YOUR BRAIN?

At its simplest level, the brain can be regarded as having three distinct sections, all of which work together (see Figure 1).

Cerebellum or the Reptilian Brain

At the base of the brain is the cerebellum or reptilian brain. It is located at the lowest part of the back of the head, just above the spinal column. As the name suggests, this is the part of the brain we have inherited from our reptilian ancestors. The cerebellum operates like an autopilot, controlling basic automatic functions such as sleeping and waking, breathing, digestion and heart functions.

Figure 1: The Triune Brain (Developed by Paul McLean)

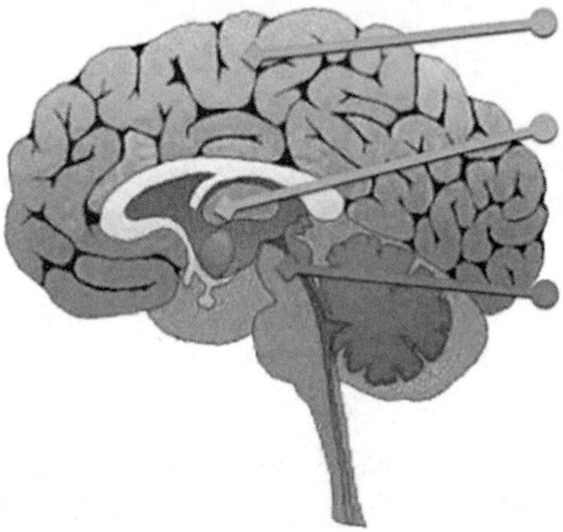

Neocortex:
Rational or
Thinking Brain

Limbic System:
Emotional or
Feeling Brain

Cerebellum:
Instinctual or
Reptilian Brain

Limbic System or the Mammalian Brain

Sitting above the cerebellum is the limbic system, often referred to as the emotional brain or mammalian brain – the part of the brain that developed with the evolution of mammals about 300 million years ago. Mammals differ from reptiles in that they give birth to immature young who are unable to survive on their own. The adult mammals (both male and female) are designed to feed and take care of their young, so that they can survive into adulthood. This evolutionary process entailed the necessity for nature to develop a way to create a bond between the parent and their young, so that they would even put themselves at risk (perhaps by going hungry) in order to ensure the survival of their young. This willingness to place themselves at risk was facilitated by the evolution of an emotional attachment and a protective instinct between parent and offspring, hence the development of emotions in mammals.

The limbic system governs our emotional responses, instinctive behaviours and basic impulses such as fear, anger, hunger, thirst and desire – instincts required for survival. It also forms a link between the other two parts of the brain, the neocortex and the cerebellum.

The emotional brain contains important areas such as the amygdala, hippocampus, hypothalamus and thalamus, all of which regulate our emotional state and are highly active when we are in a stressed state. See Chapter 15 for more information on the emotional brain.

4

The Neocortex or the 'Thinking Brain'

Finally, the top layer of the brain is a walnut-shaped structure surrounding the mammalian brain called the neocortex, or the 'new layer' of the human brain. The neocortex, which is responsible for higher-order thinking processes, is the part of the brain that, from an evolutionary perspective, developed most recently.

It is subdivided into two hemispheres (right and left). The area behind the forehead is known as the frontal lobes. The neocortex governs such functions as vision, hearing, perceptual awareness, language, consciousness, intentional movement, impulse control, decision-making, planning for the future, language, the ability to focus attention and other higher-order cognitive functions, which is why it is often referred to as the 'thinking brain'.

While all of the functions of the neocortex are important, the frontal lobes are of particular importance. Some scientists have likened this area of the brain to the conductor of an orchestra as it coordinates, promotes and suppresses the actions of the different brain areas and allows us to make plans and decisions. These lobes are active when we are contemplating our world or reflecting on ourselves, when we are empathising with others or trying to establish what they are thinking. The frontal lobes are also responsible for controlling base instincts and urges that may conflict with what is accepted in society and our own best interests. In fact, it could be said that it is this ability of the frontal lobes to self-reflect and think abstractly that separates humans from other animal species. As such, the development of these frontal lobes is hugely important in our maturation process.

The cerebellum, limbic system and neocortex portions of the brain interact with one another on a constant basis in response to what is happening in the environment. As each part gains control, we behave accordingly. It is useful to think of the emotional mammalian brain and the neocortex thinking brain as different aspects of ourselves, with the emotional brain often at odds with the more rational, considered human brain.

Much of our irrational behaviour can be understood when the interactions between the emotional brain and the thinking brain are taken into account. Remember that either one of these brains can take control and determine our response to a situation, such as extreme fear or even rage when we experience an unexpected shock. But they also work well together, giving us two differing perspectives on a situation.

Your emotional brain can be your best friend or your worst enemy. It can cause you to make decisions that are at odds with your more reasoned self. It is neither good nor bad; it is just more primitive, like the brain of an ape. Consider the following examples, which illustrate the type of tug-of-war that takes place between the thinking brain and the emotional brain:

Thinking brain: 'I need to lose weight.'
Emotional brain: 'That chocolate cake looks delicious and I *have* to have it.'

Thinking brain: 'I want to learn French.'
Emotional brain: 'It's raining outside and going to the French class means I will get cold and wet.'

Thinking brain: 'I know that what my boss just said is correct. I did make a bit of a mess of that meeting.'
Emotional brain: 'It's not fair. He's always picking on me.'

Following recent advances in brain-imaging technology, it is now possible to use brain scans to view interactions between these brain regions. For example, if you are calm and relaxed, a brain scan will show activation in the frontal area of your neocortex – as you will be thinking rationally and feel in control. Conversely, if you are feeling anxious, angry or stressed, the scan will show that activation is more concentrated in the emotional brain. This demonstrates that, depending on our state of mind, different areas of the brain become active, which explains why we respond irrationally at times, particularly when we are stressed.

Research studies carried out in the 1990s by neuroscientists Joseph LeDoux (Professor of Neuroscience and Psychology at New York University) and Antonio Damasio (Professor of Neuroscience at the University of Southern California) showed that the *emotional brain responds quicker than the thinking brain* to a situation. This explains why we may instantly react in a certain way when we are angry, frightened or hurt and that, over time – seconds, minutes, hours, days or even weeks – when we have cooled down, we can consider things in a more reasonable way and see things from another person's point of view. This is because when we have calmed down, the more reasonable, thinking part of the brain can take control and we can reflect more objectively on what has occurred.

Depending on the individual and the circumstances, the degree to which we can calm our emotional brain and access our thinking brain will determine how wise our reactions or responses will be in any given situation. This is doubly true for children of all ages. Think of the screaming toddler having a tantrum in a supermarket. Toddlers have little or no control over their emotional brain, and so they become a bag of emotions, full of rage, fear or sadness. It is only when they have had reassurance from an adult, and have calmed down, that it is possible to reason somewhat with them. As children grow older, this capacity to manage their emotional brain develops, and their ability to calm themselves increases.

However, as we know, some adults never manage to develop this skill. They are still controlled by their emotional responses. Teenagers, on the other hand, are in the process of developing this skill, and due to the fact that they are also dealing with additional hormones and brain changes, it can seem as if they have lost whatever control they had and are now going backwards. Fear not! They are not going backwards; they are just dealing with more stressors now than they have had to deal with to date.

2

HUMAN GIVENS – EMOTIONAL NEEDS

The ability to calm ourselves and access our wiser, thinking brain is a skill we all develop to a greater or lesser extent. This skill is vital for good emotional health and for parenting. Recent research shows that the ability to put yourself in someone else's shoes and see things from their perspective is one of the most important skills in parenting. And you can only do this when you yourself are calm, and are not in a stressed state.

Achieving calmness in today's stressful world is difficult. How can you manage your teenager's emotional outbursts if you yourself are in a vulnerable, anxious or angry state? Learning to be calm and to manage your own stress requires an understanding of yourself and of your emotions. Everyone gets stressed when they feel threatened in some way, and emotional adolescents can appear threatening to any adult.

All humans – adults, teenagers and children – have certain things in common and, before exploring the difficulties that are specific to teenagers, it is useful to outline these common attributes. All humans are life forms and so have basic needs that must be met, such as food, water, shelter and oxygen. In order to ensure these needs are met, every living thing is endowed with a set of 'templates' of incomplete patterns that they instinctively seek completion of in the environment. These patterns are often expressed as 'needs'. Along with the basics of water, oxygen and nutrients – physical needs – that all living things need, animals, including humans, also have social or emotional needs. We are endowed with these templates at conception, and from the moment of birth we seek to have these needs met. If we are born into an environment that provides us with the means to get these needs met, we develop well.

It is the way that our needs are met – and the impact that life has on them – that determines the individual emotional and mental health of each person. We have been born with physical and emotional needs, and, consequently, these needs are regarded as a 'given' – hence the term 'Human Givens'. So what are the human needs that must be met, so that we can live a healthy, functioning life?

PHYSICAL NEEDS

We have always instinctively understood that given the right amounts of healthy air, food, water, exercise, sleep and sufficient shelter, a human will be physically well. These physical needs are fairly obvious, as if they are not met we become physically unwell and eventually die. So these basic physical needs are known as 'givens'.

EMOTIONAL NEEDS

Human beings are not by nature solitary creatures; we evolved as social beings, surviving through the millennia by forming together in groups. The makeup of the group to which we belong, and with which we interact, can determine much of our emotional health, creating a sense of security and belonging, or a sense of fear and isolation. As social creatures, we have been designed to have social needs or emotional needs; these too are regarded as a 'given'. As a result, the environment from which you need to draw sustenance is not only physical, it is also social. For this reason, any human who is living in total isolation will not survive well psychologically.

The concept of emotional needs has been studied for centuries, and psychologists are very aware of the importance of having these needs met in order to live a fulfilling life. Often, we are not as aware of our emotional needs as we are of our physical needs. When we are feeling distressed or anxious, looking for a physical cause is often our first recourse. Most of us are not so in tune with seeking out, and being mindful of, what we need in order to be emotionally healthy.

So, what exactly do we mean by emotional needs? What are the prerequisites for emotional health? Over the last century, psychologists have identified emotional needs for humans; such needs include:

- A need for security
- A need for giving and receiving attention
- A need for a sense of control and autonomy
- A need for friendship and intimacy
- A need for a connection to community
- A need for a sense of competence and achievement
- A need for privacy
- A need for status or recognition
- A need for meaning and purpose

These emotional needs hold true for all humans, children, teenagers and adults alike; moreover, our entire well-being depends on having these emotional needs met. It is useful therefore to examine them one by one in more detail.

1. *A need for security:* A safe environment, which enables you to live your life in safety without excessive or undue fear.

   At a very basic level, a human needs to feel safe, to have a sense of security in their life. As you will no doubt have observed from time to time as part of your own life experience, people who feel constantly threatened, or who are living in a violent or aggressive environment, will look anxious and edgy.

> To understand what this 'need for security' feels like, think back to a time in your life when you felt unsafe. This could have been in class with an aggressive teacher or with a group of friends who picked on you. Perhaps you were bullied at work, or felt your job was under threat. Maybe you were mugged or burgled. All of these situations can affect your level of security and leave you emotionally vulnerable.
>
> Compare these to times when you felt secure in the past, when you felt safe in your environment. Try to recall how steady you felt when you were secure. While none of us can be completely secure, a basic level of security is essential if we are to ensure our emotional well-being.

Their stress levels will be increased, as a result of their internal alarm system being on permanent alert. When this happens, their brain responds to the perceived or real threat by triggering what psychologists call the 'stress response'.

When the 'stress response' is activated, the levels of the stress hormones cortisol and adrenaline are increased in your body, causing knock-on effects that can affect your physical body as well as your behaviour and your thinking. This in turn affects your immune system, concentration, memory, sleep and ability to learn, among other things.

2. *A need for giving and receiving attention:* Attention is a form of emotional nutrition that fuels the development of each individual, family and culture.

Humans need to give and receive attention. Babies come into the world needing attention, and we instinctively give them that attention. We look into their little faces and speak to them and, even though they don't understand what we are saying, they experience receiving attention. Within a short period of time, they begin to give us back attention in the form of smiles and gurgles. This exchange of attention creates a bond between the baby and their caregivers.

Attention creates the basic feeling that someone is interested in you and wants to know about you (i.e. what you are like and so on), and it also gives you a sense of identity. Children who are starved of attention, but are otherwise physically nourished, do not develop well cognitively (i.e. intellectually) because the brain requires a certain level of attention and interaction in order to develop properly. Researchers have found ample evidence of poor cognitive development in children who were brought up in poorly run orphanages, where the level of attention paid to the children was far from sufficient. (In fact, the modern habit of using a television screen to babysit small children has been shown to negatively affect the development of crucial brain functions and, as such, it is now recommended by paediatricians that children younger than five are not given access to television at all, and then only limited access beyond the age of five.) The same principle holds true for adults; if we don't receive sufficient attention, we become lonely, isolated and depressed.

Not only do we need to receive attention, we also need to give attention to others. In fact, what is needed is a balanced exchange of attention. Giving a child too much attention can result in giving them an expectation of being entitled to masses of attention, and the child can subsequently grow into an attention-seeking adult. Too little attention also causes problems: when a person has been starved of attention as a child, they may accept any attention that is offered, thereby leaving themselves open to numerous possible negative consequences. Such people can become prey to unscrupulous individuals or groups who exploit their need for attention, by manipulating them through giving and withholding attention.

Can you think of a time when your attention needs were not being met? When you felt ignored or unheard, felt lonely or on the outside? Compare this with a time when your attention needs were being met, when you were listened to, and heard, when your views were being acknowledged, when someone was genuinely interested in you.

3. *A need for a sense of control and autonomy:* In other words, being able to make decisions and choices for ourselves, and being able to direct our lives and have control over what happens to us.

    A need for a sense of control and autonomy begins early in life. For example, a child of between six and nine months will attempt to hold their own bottle, and a toddler will begin to assert their own authority by becoming adept at shouting 'no' – refusing many things, even things they may actually want and delight in. Such is their need to exert control that 'no' is frequently a child's first response until they reach a stage where they are comfortable that they have a certain amount of control and they can exercise choice – both a 'yes' and a 'no'. The need for control increases as a child develops, and by the teenage years it is often this need that is the greatest source of conflict between parents and teenagers.

    Punishment often involves taking away people's sense of control: we ground young people, we imprison criminals so that they cannot choose when or what to eat, when to exercise, and so on. Often, we unwittingly do the same in our institutions. In order to create a well-run hospital, school or nursing home, we take away control from the residents or students, which may then create people who find it difficult to make decisions on their own, or to deal effectively with the world. The lack of control and autonomy eventually disempowers them and may lead to them becoming institutionalised.

Think back to times when your wishes were not being taken into account, when you felt 'out of control'. Perhaps you were a passenger in a car and the driver was going too fast, or driving aggressively. Or perhaps there was an occasion when you were ill in hospital and felt at the mercy of medical staff. Or maybe you were in a work situation where you were dependent on someone else, and they were in a more powerful position than you.

We feel out of control when something or someone else is dictating to us and giving us no choice.

When we have too much on our plate, and we are overwhelmed, we may feel that we are 'not in control'. Conversely, we become calm and feel good when we finally get things sorted out and we feel 'back in control again'. Control is inexorably linked to the need for security; when we feel out of control we feel very insecure.

However, like all needs, control needs to be in balance. Too much control (which often stems from either an insecurity or a need for power over others) is also not healthy. It puts us in danger of becoming a 'control freak'. What we need is just the right amount – some control but not complete control.

4. *A need for friendship and intimacy:* This is often expressed as knowing at least one person who accepts us totally for who we are, 'warts and all'.

   When this need is not met and we feel alone and friendless, it can cause great anxiety and loneliness. It often occurs with the death of a beloved partner, family member or best friend; it may also follow separation or divorce. This loss can be very difficult, as we make the necessary adjustments to a new reality without our soulmate or best friend, and also as we attempt to establish new friendships.

Think back to a time when you felt alone or lonely. Maybe you had lost a friend or a partner through separation, emigration or death. Perhaps someone had rejected you for some reason, either valid or invalid.

We all need at least one good friend, and such friendship can take time to develop when we have lost someone important in our lives.

Emotional intimacy and acceptance of who we are gives us a sense of security in ourselves. Being connected to others who are of like mind – who appreciate us and value us even though we are flawed – insulates us from the world, which can be a cruel and brutally honest place, especially when we are young and our egos are fragile and developing.

5. *A need for a connection to community:* Sometimes referred to as a need for belonging, being part of social groups outside our immediate family, as after all we are social beings.

Think back to a time when you were not part of 'the group'. Perhaps it was your first day in a new job, or in a place where you knew no one. Or maybe you moved to a new country, school or university.

Being outside the group can give us a sense of isolation and aloneness. It can also leave us feeling vulnerable and insecure as it takes time to become part of a group. In fact, isolating someone is one of the tactics that is used to control us. One such example is the rejection of a whistleblower or 'sending someone to Coventry' as a means of punishing a person for their behaviour.

Perhaps you can also recall a time when you really felt part of a group. Being accepted as a member of a family, sports club, church, book club, work team, or any other type of grouping can really enhance our sense of well-being.

In prehistoric times, being alone in the world meant you were prey to wild animals or to other exploitative humans. We survived through the millennia by being part of a group, and, consequently, we have evolved to need this sense of belonging. Being part of a group or community gives us that sense of belonging and security, which can help us reduce stress and feel more secure in the world.

The need for a connection to a community is very much related to the need for emotional intimacy. In fact, all nine emotional needs are interrelated, as each can impact on the others.

6. *A need for a sense of competence and achievement:* A feeling that we are achieving something, and are competent in at least one area of our life, which in turn builds our self-esteem.

Stretching ourselves to achieve a goal, or learning something new that increases our competence, can give us the natural 'high' of achievement, which is a feeling quite unlike anything else. Consider, for example, a child learning to walk or run, and how proud he is of himself. He has reached a goal that he has been striving for. Children will naturally push themselves to the next goal, in order to continue growing and learning. It is this need that has enabled the human race to achieve all that it has achieved over the millennia. Consider too the natural cycle of learning, starting with the curiosity or the realisation that there is a skill or an ability we would like to master – perhaps driving a car or learning a language. It begins with an initial feeling of incompetence: 'I don't think I can do this.' All real achievement requires effort, and we are rewarded with a natural 'high' when we stretch ourselves and achieve something we set out to do.

Think back to a time when you were bored, completing mundane tasks that didn't stretch you. Now, think of a time when you set out to achieve a goal, put in effort and subsequently achieved that goal. This achievement was almost certainly rewarded with a good feeling and a sense of pride in yourself.

Achieving something and becoming competent is the one sure way to increase balanced self-esteem, as your sense of self is then based on reality and not on someone else's perception of you, be that a highly positive or a highly negative perception.

7. *A need for privacy:* Time and space to yourself to reflect and consolidate your own experience.

While we all need to be part of a group, we also need time out, away from the world, to reflect on ourselves and on our experiences. This allows us to develop our sense of identity as separate individuals. We can see this development naturally throughout childhood, starting with the need to go to the bathroom on our own, to dress in private or to create a diary where we can retreat into our own private world.

The need for privacy increases with the years, and as an individual develops and grows, so does their need for privacy. Like all emotional needs, the extent of this need varies from person to person. A person's need for time to themselves should be respected. For example, some people are more naturally introverted and will require more time on their own than might be the case for their extroverted colleagues. For these people, spending too much time with others can be difficult and stressful.

> If you have ever been in a situation where someone opened your post or read your emails or text messages without your permission, or rummaged through your private documents or other personal papers, then you have experienced your need for privacy being violated.
>
> Alternatively, you might recall a time when you spent too long a period with other people while on a holiday or on a trip abroad. This feeling of needing to spend time alone is the need for privacy. This need often becomes very acute in the teenage years, causing parents and adults a significant increase in worry.

8. *A need for status or recognition:* A sense that we are accepted and valued in the various social groupings to which we belong.

   In the context of this particular meaning of the word, status does not necessarily mean high status. It means that we are recognised for who we are and what we do, the part we play in society. Are you an expert on plants or baking? Is technology, photography or football one of your key skills? Are you the funny one who makes everyone laugh? We all need status or recognition in some form or another, and all good teachers and parents will therefore acknowledge the natural talents and skills of young people; this gives them status or recognition among their peers.

> Think back to a time when you did not feel recognised for some talent or achievement. How did that feel? Or worse still, if someone else took credit and achieved recognition for *your* work?

9. *A need for meaning and purpose:* We all need to feel that life has meaning in some way; among other things, it helps us to cope when times are difficult.

   If all of our other emotional needs are met but this one is not, we may feel that life is meaningless, which can be hugely debilitating. A life without meaning can be a very disillusioning experience; indeed, it is often this need that can occupy the minds of reflective young people, as they increasingly become aware of the shallowness of the world and look for something more worthwhile and meaningful.

   It can be difficult to articulate what exactly gives our lives meaning and purpose, but, in general, when we feel we are part of something bigger than ourselves, we get a feeling that life has meaning. We feel this when we are needed by others, for example through a job such as a nurse or a teacher, or being a member of a team working on a project. Or we might feel needed as a sibling, parent or friend. When others need us, we have a sense of meaning, and a sense that there is a reason for our existence.

   We also get a sense of meaning when we are stretching ourselves and growing. When we are working towards a goal or a solution and are making progress – such as in a sport or through study, e.g. running a marathon, being involved in research or acquiring new knowledge or a new skill.

   Having an overriding philosophical perspective on life – be that a spiritual sense, or a particular philosophy or outlook – can give us a feeling that we are part of something bigger than ourselves. So being a member of a social organisation that is working to make other people's lives better by protecting the planet, or volunteering with a charity, gives us a sense of being part of something bigger than ourselves, and also give us a sense of meaning and purpose.

Have you ever experienced periods when you found it difficult to find meaning in life? We sometimes feel this way when we are a bit depressed, and feel there is no point in life. Or sometimes it happens to people who have achieved a great deal, for example if they have created a major business, or acquired a lot of wealth, but nonetheless life seems empty.

These questions often don't arise in our normal day-to-day lives, rather, it is at life's major turning points (such as adolescence or mid-life, or during times of crisis) that they come to the fore.

Life has meaning when we see our actions as valuable and important. In fact, our lives have meaning whenever we instil value into whatever task or activity we are engaged in, or in the way we are leading our lives.

The needs listed above are our innate, basic emotional needs, and all humans have these needs, whether they are eight months or eighty years old. We come into the world with these innate but as yet unmet needs. How well they are met in the world determines many aspects of our personality and our character, how well we develop physically and emotionally, how we interact with other people, and what we achieve in life. If these needs are met in a fairly balanced way, we feel that life is good. In truth, we cannot be mentally unwell if all our emotional needs are being met in balance.

However, if our emotional needs are not being met, we soon get frustrated, stressed and angry. If this continues for a long time, it can lead us to develop one or more of a range of disturbing psychological states, such as anxiety disorders, depression or addiction. Furthermore, our psychologically and emotionally disturbed behaviour impacts on those around us – family, friends, colleagues and the wider community.

One particularly useful exercise to do is to complete an Emotional Needs Audit on yourself and consider the ways in which you can improve your own life and get your needs met more healthily. You will find a copy of this audit on page 144.

3

Human Givens – Innate Guidance System

Innate Guidance System

Our emotional needs are only half the story. Apart from having to take nourishment from the environment in the form of physical and emotional needs, we also share another commonality with all other living things. All life forms have an intelligence of some sort; this intelligence assists them in getting their needs met. Plants 'know' to grow towards sunlight, and mammals instinctively know how to suckle from birth. We are all born with an 'innate guidance system' that directs us towards the nourishment we need in order to thrive. This innate guidance system comprises a wealth of resources and it is the unique composition and configuration of this system within each of us that contributes towards the development of our personality and temperament. The resources that make up our innate guidance system include:

- A complex and long-term memory
- The ability to build rapport and to connect with others
- Emotions and instincts
- An imagination
- A conscious, rational mind
- The ability to 'know' through pattern-matching
- A dreaming brain
- An observing self

Each of us has these resources in some form or other, with some resources being more developed than others. Some people have a great imagination whereas others have a well-developed rational mind or a good memory. This is what makes each of us unique. Each resource has a unique function to perform and they work together to help ensure our emotional needs are met. As children grow and become teenagers and adults, these resources develop and become more refined and mature.

So what are these resources?

1. *A complex and long-term memory:* A complex and long-term memory allows us to add to our innate knowledge and learn from our experience. Memory gives us access to prior experience, which helps us understand the world; this in turn enables us to meet our needs. Memory assists us by developing a bank of learning and experience, which enables us to negotiate our way in the world more effectively.

   We understand the importance of memory from people who have lost the ability to lay down new memories. One such case is that of Henry Molaison, whose brain operation in 1953 – carried out in an attempt to cure his epilepsy – left him unable to form new memories. In other words, he could remember events from before his operation but he was unable to remember anything that happened after that point. Even though his doctors treated him for over 30 years, they had to be reintroduced to him every time they met. For the rest of his life, Henry was unable to function in the world; he could not look after himself or hold down a job, and he remained completely dependent on others. In fact, the surgeon who performed Henry's operation spent much of his subsequent career campaigning against this procedure.

   While memory is vital for learning, so is the ability to forget. We need the ability to learn from difficult situations, and be able to put such situations behind us and get on with life. Constantly digging up and dwelling on painful memories can affect both our mood and our emotional health.

2. *The ability to build rapport and connect with others:* The ability to build rapport with other people is necessary for relationships and to empathise with others. It enables us to meet our need for friendship, intimacy and attention exchange, and to have a sense of belonging to a group or community.

This ability to build connections is innate in all healthy humans, and is present from the moment a baby is born. A baby's chances of surviving and thriving are boosted by the ability to build a connection with an adult caregiver. When a healthy baby is only a few hours old, they will try to make a connection by copying another human. They will respond to signals from that human face through 'mirroring' those expressions. All healthy babies do this.

3. *Emotions and instincts:* These have evolved to help us survive. They give us information on how we perceive our environment. So, when we perceive that we are being threatened, we trigger the stress or 'fight or flight' response, and our bodies become flooded with cortisol and adrenaline (more on this in later chapters), thus causing us to become fearful or angry and feel that we need to defend ourselves.

While these emotions and instincts give us information based on our perception of reality, they are not always accurate. Consider, for example, how you might feel if you were walking alone down a dark, poorly lit street late at night and you heard footsteps close behind you. While you might suddenly become very fearful and expect the worst, that fear would subside when you saw your supposed attacker turning in the gate of his house and heading to his front door.

In other words, emotions and instincts are vital for your survival, and they need to be acknowledged and taken seriously. But we also need to check them against additional information that can either validate or negate your initial perception. Emotions and instincts need to be processed by your rational mind in order to respond most appropriately.

4. *An imagination:* Imagination is a very powerful tool. When it is used positively, it can help us test out solutions to a particular problem by mentally rehearsing them. It is the basis of creativity and invention; without it, you cannot dream up possibilities to solve problems or new ways to improve your life.

Albert Einstein is often quoted on this topic: 'Imagination is more important than knowledge. For knowledge is limited to all we now know and understand, while imagination embraces the entire world, and all there ever will be to know and understand.'

However, misuse of imagination can cause serious problems. For example, some people become very stressed when they remember hurts that they have received in the past, and then imagine that they might be hurt in a similar way in the future. Others can make themselves anxious or depressed by imagining all kinds of catastrophic or miserable outcomes for themselves in the future. It is far more productive to use your imagination to build on your past experiences and knowledge to come up with inspired, intelligent solutions than it is to imagine emotionally arousing scenarios of all the dreadful things that could happen.

5. *A conscious, rational mind:* Having a conscious, rational mind gives us the ability to stand back from our emotional responses, check them out and make positive decisions. It helps us problem-solve. In order to do this, we must be able to calm our emotional reactions so that we can think rationally about the situation in hand and engage our imagination positively and creatively. By doing this, it will help us to think about our problems rationally and find solutions to our problems. This might mean that we need to let go of past hurts and consider various options, so that we can take constructive action and make good changes in our lives.

6. *The ability to 'know' through pattern-matching:* Pattern-matching or recognition (which is closely linked to the part of the brain that controls memory) is the process by which we recognise and understand the world. Specifically, it is the activity that our brain engages in whenever we perceive something new or familiar – and through which we give meaning to what we perceive.

   Our brain pattern-matches a current perception with a similar experience in the past. It unconsciously asks the simple question 'What is this like?' and comes up with a similar match. For example, if you were to come across an exotic, bright-yellow fruit that you have never seen before, your brain would go on an internal search to find an approximate match and you might then describe it as: 'It's a bit like a lemon.' In response, your brain would generate an expectation based on that particular exotic fruit/lemon pattern-match. So, if you were then to take a bite of this new, exotic fruit, you might expect it to taste like a lemon.

   Or, if you encountered something unusual like a chair suspended by wire from a ceiling, the pattern-matching mechanism in your brain will bestow the *meaning* of 'chair' onto the suspended chair even though it doesn't look like most chairs, which have four legs and are on the ground: in other words, it will recognise it as an object that someone would use for sitting on. (For more on pattern-matching see Chapter 4.)

Many of the ways in which we are influenced exploit this pattern-matching mechanism in the brain. Another way of seeing it is that the brain unconsciously takes a pattern or a rule that has worked well in the past and applies it to what *appears to be* a similar situation in the present. It takes a short cut, as it were – something that can be very useful when it is applied correctly. An example of this in practice is to be found in the image in Figure 2. Check it out for yourself: do you see the dog?

Figure 2: Pattern-Matching

As you switch from seeing just dots to seeing a dog, you are activating a different pattern-match and ascribing a different meaning in each case.

Unless you are aware and reasonably calm, it can be difficult to question and analyse these unconscious pattern-matches, and ensure that your perceptions are accurate. Only then can you make a conscious decision regarding what you see and how you should react to a situation or problem.

7. *A dreaming brain:* Sleep and dreaming are vital to our well-being, and although it may look like not much is happening while we are sleeping, our brains are working hard to ensure that we process what we have learned during the day, and incorporate that new information into the knowledge we have already there. But why do we dream, and what function does it serve?

   One of the reasons we dream at night is to process and discharge emotions that were not acted out during the day. Take, for example, a situation where you were really angry with a work colleague or a family member but, for various reasons, it might not have been wise to explode and tell them what you thought of them. So you supress these thoughts, and the physical and mental effects of the angry, emotional thoughts need to be diffused and discharged later that night. We process these supressed emotions by dreaming. In our dreams we create a metaphorical representation of the emotionally arousing situation (like a play on a stage) and allow it to be acted out safely, without creating serious consequences for our careers or our family lives. So, after a day of suppressed frustration at work or at home you may have a dream where you find yourself shouting at or punching people – the instinctive reactions that you were obliged to suppress earlier.

8. *An observing self:* This is our self-awareness, the part of ourselves that allows us to separate ourselves from our emotions and thoughts, to be more objective, and to recognise ourselves as a unique centre of awareness.

   The so-called 'observing self' is the most complex and advanced function of the brain. It helps us to reflect and to respond rather than react. You can use it to reflect, for example, on your emotions, such as 'Why was I so anxious at school/work today?' or 'Why am I so irritated with my children lately?' or on thoughts such as 'Why do I think I am not appreciated at work, given that I have just been promoted?'

The observing self helps us to consciously consider our perceptions, feelings and thoughts, and to check their validity. All healthy people have the ability to detach from their thoughts, emotions and behaviours, and reflect on themselves and their responses. This ability is facilitated by the need for privacy, because it is only by taking time out by yourself that you can reflect and develop that part of yourself that can be more objective.

These resources of the 'innate guidance system' are also 'givens' – different aspects of our intelligence that assist us in getting our needs met. This innate guidance system has undergone continuous refinement and development over the millennia and its unique composition and make-up contributes to the development and personality of each individual.

The 'human givens' – i.e. the innate guidance system and physical and emotional needs we are born with – can be thought of as an interconnected framework, within which we use our guidance system to get our needs met. All our behaviour (however irrational) is an attempt to have these needs met. Our emotional health is determined by how well our needs are met in balance, and how we utilise our innate guidance system.

When you feel emotionally fulfilled and are operating effectively in the world, you are more likely to be mentally healthy and stable. But, when too many of your physical and emotional needs are not met, or when your innate guidance system is being misused – either unwittingly or otherwise – you suffer considerable distress. And so do the people around you.

4

UNDERSTANDING HOW OUR BRAIN LEARNS

We are what we learn and an understanding of how we learn can greatly assist us in understanding ourselves. Scientists previously believed that the brain stopped developing when a child reached the age of ten (which is when the brain reaches its maximum physical size) and that after that age the brain remained a static organ, with fixed abilities. We now know that this information is incorrect. The brain is, in fact, a highly dynamic and malleable organ that changes in response to every new experience we encounter or every new activity we engage in. It is also shaped by repetition: just as particular muscles in the body respond and grow as a result of repeated use and exercise, our brain also grows in response to repeated use. This brain plasticity phenomenon applies equally to children, teenagers and adults.

The cells in the brain (known as neurons) are constantly changing and making new connections – a process that is designed to assist us in learning and growing, and thus serve us better. So, as we recite lines of poetry, or memorise multiplication tables, French verbs or the lyrics of a song, what we are actually doing is building neuronal networks or patterns in exactly the same way we did when we were very young and first learned to hold a bottle, take our first steps, ride a bike or kick a football.

As adults, we know from experience that if we practise tasks and repeat them, they become easier, and even become automatic. For example, cast your mind back to the effort you put into learning something new, such as driving a car. As you will recall from your days as a learner driver, initially it took tremendous effort and concentration to get all the various steps involved into the right sequence. But with time and practice, it became a series of unconscious steps.

When your brain is acquiring a new skill, repeating the learning steps over and over creates and embeds neuronal patterns for that skill. This pattern-making process is the same for everything you have ever learned in your life from the time you were a baby: distinguishing your mother's voice from that of others, grasping an object, crawling, walking, running, speaking, reading, writing. All of these tasks were learned and accomplished in the same way – by the brain's neurons self-organising and forming patterns once they had learned a task sufficiently well, at which point carrying out the task became automatic, and the learning became embedded in the neuronal pathways.

In short, your brain develops patterns based on what you have *experienced*, and those patterns then create an expectation of what you predict will happen in the future. The neuronal pathways have become primed or programmed to automatically expect what has occurred previously. Conversely, when the brain encounters something new and unfamiliar, it perceives the new input as unexpected or disturbing, simply because it doesn't fit with the neuronal pathways that we have already laid down. For example, imagine what your response would be if, when you pressed the brakes of your car, the car didn't slow down. This new 'disturbing' information would lead to a reorganisation of the existing brain pattern. As a result of the reorganisation caused by the unnerving experience of faulty brakes, you might subsequently test the brakes of your car every time you set out on a journey. This might continue for weeks, months or years – depending on how unnerved you were by the original event. Aspects of your innate guidance system (brain) have now changed. Your pattern-matching function and memory have been altered by this experience, giving you access to knowledge you did not have until now.

Continuing the car analogy: imagine an inexperienced driver's first encounter with driving on an icy road. In this case, the person's brain has formed the expectation that *steering* to the left will result in the car *veering* to the left. The problem is, however, that in icy road conditions, the car's behaviour would not match the learner driver's expectations. As in the case of the brakes example above, the person's original brain pattern would be disturbed, and if the car subsequently headed for a wall instead of heading in the direction in which the person was steering, they would experience such an event as a shock.

Not surprisingly, we pay close attention to information that falls into the shock category. In the case of the icy road example, we incorporate the newly acquired information about the way the car steering responds in such conditions into the 'driving pattern' part of our brain. In other words, our brain pattern has now been expanded to include these possibilities as a result of these two frightening incidents. This dynamic learning process allows us to incorporate new information following each new experience. In this way, we embellish our brain and become wiser and better able to negotiate the world.

As the above examples illustrate, our perception of events involves a lot more than merely capturing and storing an incoming stimulus. It also involves creating an expectation of knowing what is about to confront us and enables us to prepare for it. Without these expectations based on past experiences, we would perceive each experience as a new one and this would completely overwhelm us. But there is more to this process than merely creating expectations. Depending on the expectation that is triggered by the pattern, we will trigger a corresponding *emotion* based on that expectation. Going back to the driving analogy: following the initial experience with the icy road, the driver may now experience great fear at the prospect of driving in freezing temperatures. What this all shows is that the brain's neural networks respond in a pattern that is established by past experience. The more often a specific pattern is generated or activated, the more embedded the pattern becomes. Previous input shapes the way we experience the next input. As a consequence, it is no exaggeration to state that *after* we have an experience we are not the same person we were *before* that experience. Experience changes perception.

PERCEPTION AND REALITY

Our perception creates our world and our reality and, as such, it is very important. If we return once more to the driving example, we can use this analogy to explain an acronym that has been used to describe the pattern-activating and expectation process that determines perception.

Joe Griffin, co-founder of the Human Givens approach, first described it in the late 1990s using the acronym APET. The 'A' in APET stands for 'activating agent', a stimulus from the environment (which in the case of the learner driver example is ice). The activating agent 'ice' triggers a neural pattern in the brain (hence the 'P' for 'pattern-match'). The pattern triggered (which could be a fun experience or a fearful one, depending on the individual in question) creates an expectation, which in turn gives rise to an associated emotion 'E' (in this case either fun and delight, or fear and dread). The emotion triggered will inspire thoughts 'T' (although this is not always the case). Any subsequent thoughts will be coloured by the emotions produced, and will be either positive thoughts of anticipation (such as 'This will be great fun!') or negative, catastrophic thoughts (such as 'I won't be able to manage this. I'm sure I'll crash the car!')

So:

In Person A, the APET sequence might unfold as follows:

A = Activating agent — Ice
P = Pattern-match (past experience/expectation) — Fun
E = Expectation triggers an emotion — Excitement
T = Thought — 'This will be great fun.'

In contrast, in Person B the APET sequence might unfold as follows:

A = Activating agent — Ice
P = Pattern-match (past experience/expectation) — Crash
E = Expectation triggers an emotion — Fear
T = Thought — 'I'm going to crash.'

ASK YOURSELF

Think back to a particular occasion when you experienced a strong emotion, stronger than would have seemed warranted at the time. Now use the APET framework to analyse and reflect on this reaction and see if you can ascertain the pattern-match. Identifying and naming the pattern-match can in itself reduce the automatic emotional reaction, and give you a greater sense of control over your own reactions to situations.

The APET model illustrates how the brain works in the generation of perception. It is useful to keep this model of perception in mind not only when you are thinking about problems in relation to teenagers, but also when you are thinking of challenging situations that you may have to deal with yourself.

These pattern-matches occur in the limbic system, the emotional brain, and they generate automatic thoughts. These thoughts may or may not be appropriate. An intense fear of spiders can create irrational thoughts that we are going to die. If the emotion generated is not too strong, we can question our automatic thoughts and change them. If it is intense (as it may be when a person has a phobia), this will not be possible at that time. The person has been emotionally hijacked and cannot think clearly. Once they have calmed down, they are able to consider the situation more rationally and realise that the spider will not kill them.

It can be a great relief to sufferers of irrational phobias to learn that a more primitive part of the brain has taken over and that they are not 'foolish'; rather, their reaction is just an expectation that their brain has been conditioned to generate. Depending on the strength of the emotions triggered as a result of the APET process, corresponding thoughts will be generated. For example, a strong emotion of fear, anger or desire will cause you to have very black-and-white thoughts, which, if you were in a calmer frame of mind, might not be so extreme.

Consider the following thoughts, some of which may be familiar:

Fear:	I will *die* if he breaks off our relationship.
Anger:	I'm *never* going to speak to her again.
Terror:	The spider will *kill* me.
Desire:	I just *have* to have that doughnut.

The fear (of rejection) in the emotional brain generates the thought: 'I'll die if he breaks off our relationship,' whereas once you calm down, you may see the situation differently, perhaps less dramatically and maybe more positively. Similarly, the anger (in response to being rejected) that is generated in the emotional brain creates the thought 'I'm *never* going to speak to her again.' Again, once you calm down, you may see the other person's point of view and feel less angry about her behaviour.

These fearful or angry thoughts are generated as a result of the strength of the emotional response to a particular incident. Remembering that such thoughts are not reality – they are just thoughts generated at a point in time – this can again help you to react more appropriately and not be controlled by your emotional reactions.

EMOTIONAL AROUSAL AND CONFLICT

If you now consider a situation where you and your teenager are having a confrontation, you may recognise that some of the arguments between the two of you are, in fact, two emotional brains rowing with each other, neither making much sense, neither even listening to the other.

Consider a situation where you are simply fed up because you have just picked up, for the umpteenth time, discarded clothes, takeaway food containers or other debris generated by your teenager – a situation that triggers anger in you. As a result of this anger, your emotional brain hijacks your rational brain and you tell them in no uncertain terms what you think of their behaviour. In this case, your anger has catapulted you into the 'fight' aspect of the 'fight or flight' stress response. Simultaneously, your teenager feels under attack, catapulting them into a corresponding 'fight or flight' response, and instantly goes into defensive mode by either fighting back or storming out (perhaps slamming the door behind them).

Emotional arousal (particularly when it is high, as in the case of the parent–teenager confrontation described above) can make you blind to a bigger reality. This holds true whether the emotion is anger and rage at how we have been wronged, fear/paranoia that others are out to get us, or desire for another person (such as when you fall in love).

The Good News about Emotional Arousal

Emotions are not all bad or distorting and, without emotions, life would be colourless and bland. Emotions make you aware of being alive; they create many of the highs and lows of life. As we grow and mature, we develop a greater ability to manage our own emotions. We develop the skill of integrating emotions – even strong emotions – into our thinking, so that we are not overwhelmed by every single emotion, and can thus utilise the intelligence and capability of our rational mind.

Learning to manage your own emotional brain can go a long way towards keeping things calm, and can also help improve communication between you and your teenager (or any other adult for that matter). The various changes that take place in the brain during adolescence enhance this ability, so that by the time they reach adulthood a teenager will have become steadier and more reasonable. These changes help us feel emotions and then express them in a socially acceptable manner. You will find a number of simple techniques to help you do this in the section 'Tools for Managing Stress' in Chapter 15.

Part II

UNDERSTANDING TEENAGERS

5

Teenagers – What Is Adolescence?

Adolescence is the stage of life when a young person is undergoing the changes that are necessary to prepare them for adulthood. The purpose of this unique period is to create independence and the changes that teenagers are undergoing are designed to develop just this – an independent human being. The parents' job at this time is to support these changes and to make themselves redundant within a few years.

While this is often a very confusing stage for teenagers and adults alike, some knowledge of what is occurring, and why, can help in navigating these years. Parents often dread the adolescent years, perhaps already knowing that the strategies that worked so well up to now in terms of managing their son or daughter will no longer have the same effect. But it is not a stage to be feared, and having more information and knowledge will help you feel more competent and calm your anxieties.

Not all teenagers are the same, as every parent who has more than one child knows. But all teenagers need to negotiate their way through this stage in life and they will all do it in their own way, in their own style. The relationship between parent and teenager is often cast by the media as adversarial, and stereotypes of teenagers are misleading and not very useful. Having parents and teenagers view each other as the enemy is really not very helpful.

During the adolescent years, the brain goes through many changes. Chapter 7 explains these changes in more detail. An understanding of these physical changes in the brain – and how important they are for the development of the individual – can help you guide your teenager through these years more effectively.

If you are new to the process of managing an adolescent, it may be helpful to try the following:

> Try to recall your perception of your own parents during your teenage years. Do you remember just how frustrating they were? How your parents were always restricting you and didn't seem to realise just how intelligent and capable you were? Try to remember what you yourself were like – how confusing the world was, how self-conscious you were or how unjust life seemed to be.

Remembering your own experience can help you step into your child's shoes and see things from their perspective as you attempt to guide them through this whirlwind time, when hormones are racing, and behaviour and emotions are unpredictable. This is a period when they are discovering who they are, and it is during this time that they will gradually shape themselves into the adults they will eventually become.

One of our most common misunderstandings, as adults, is that we expect teenagers to be capable of acting like adults. This expectation in itself is frequently the basis of conflict. In reality, the teenager's brain is in the middle of a huge transition, and they are not yet capable of responsible adult behaviour. This does not mean that you should passively accept everything your teenagers do, taking the position of 'they cannot help it'; such an attitude would do them a great disservice. Instead, what is required is an acknowledgement that teenagers need direction and assistance from us parents in order to help them become responsible adults capable of all that is expected of adults in society.

In the following chapters we will explore the changes that are occurring, and how they help to explain some of the common problems that arise in the parent–teenager relationship.

WHAT DOES ADOLESCENCE MEAN?

The term 'adolescence' was coined by the American psychologist Granville Stanley Hall, who first used it about 100 years ago. He referred to it as a period of 'storm and stress', characterised by conflict with parents, mood disruptions and risky behaviour. Thus, the concept of a specific transitional stage of development between childhood and adulthood was born.

The Difference between Puberty and Adolescence

People often use the terms 'puberty' and 'adolescence' interchangeably, but there is a difference between the two. Puberty is the development of adult sexual characteristics: breasts, menstrual cycle, pubic hair, voice changes, facial hair and so on. All of these are outward signs of puberty, whereas adolescence is characterised by internal and behavioural changes. In terms of the age of onset of puberty, this varies a great deal, with some children starting early (i.e. at age 8 in girls and 9 in boys) while others take their time (i.e. as late as age 14 or 15).

With the onset of adolescence, children begin to separate from their parents. They become increasingly aware of how they are regarded by their peers, and they desperately try to fit in with whatever their peers are involved in or believe in. They begin to explore different looks and identities, and they become acutely self-conscious and aware of how they compare with others. They seek out independence and develop views of their own – views that are often at odds with those of their parents.

The progress from child brain to adolescent brain and, finally, to adult brain is, in fact, a neurologically driven process, the aim of which is to transition from the dependence of childhood to the independence of adulthood. These changes help young people prepare to leave the nest and develop the new skills and resources they will need in order to live independently as adults.

What We Now Know about the Teenage Brain

Recent advances in neuroscience have shown that the brain is constantly evolving, constantly learning, and that it is a dynamic organ being moulded and shaped by interactions between the person and the outside world. These advances have helped us understand the differences between the adult, child and adolescent brain. Having some knowledge of these differences – as well as knowledge about the physical changes the brain is undergoing (and *why* these changes are taking place) – can greatly assist adults to help younger people develop healthy behaviours and prevent them from damaging their brains unduly.

THE FALLOUT AS WELL AS THE POSITIVES

Teenagers' drive for autonomy can be confusing and exasperating for parents and teenagers, and it often results in conflicts that are characterised by 'attitude': sighs, sarcasm, tantrums, brooding silences and so on.

But, on the positive side, adolescence is also a time of intense growth – not only physically but also morally and intellectually. It is a period of self-discovery and personal growth, when teenagers learn to take care of themselves and make their own decisions. Part of this process involves making what are sometimes unwise decisions, and then having to deal with the consequences. As a parent, it is important that you ensure your teenager does deal with these consequences, rather than rushing to 'fix' the problem.

Another positive is that teenagers tend to have a clear perspective on life, often cutting through some of the mumbo-jumbo of our complex world, stating the obvious like a breath of fresh air. Their deep sense of what is fair and right can often be challenging to those of us who have learned to accept 'the way things are'.

Teenagers need to explore the world and socialise with their peers in order to learn and grow. The friends they make at this time may become very important and influential. Together, they may form close bonds, which may last throughout their lives, as they share their dreams, hopes and secrets with one another and not necessarily with their parents or teachers.

6

TEENAGERS – EMOTIONAL NEEDS, A QUESTION OF BALANCE

As outlined in Chapters 2 and 3, all humans have physical and emotional needs and an innate guidance system to help them meet these needs. This holds true for adults, children and teenagers alike. Teenagers have the same needs as adults; the only difference is that their innate guidance system, i.e. their brain, is still developing and growing. They do not have the ability to manage this innate guidance system in the same way that adults do: teenagers' ability to calm their emotional brain and reflect on their emotions and actions is still developing at this point in their lives.

As previously mentioned, all behaviour (however irrational) is an attempt to have a need met and some of the emotional needs become more pronounced as your child moves into adolescence. For example, a teenager's need to belong to a group (i.e. their peer group) can become much more important. Similarly, teenagers' need for status and privacy becomes increasingly important, as does the need for control as they begin to assert their independence and grow apart from their families and parents.

The drive to meet these needs can cause great conflict in a family as the teenager pushes parental and societal boundaries in order to meet their own needs. It can mean that the adults' need for security and control comes into direct conflict with some of the teenager's needs.

It can be useful to observe or reflect on a teenager's behaviour using the framework or the 'lens' of emotional needs. If there is conflict in the family, whether it is due to hogging the bathroom or something more serious such as drinking and staying out late, it can be helpful to ask yourself the following question: 'What need are they attempting to meet?' A teenager who spends ages in the bathroom preening and doing themselves up might be doing so to meet their need for status or attention, or their need to belong to a particular peer group. Drinking and staying out late may simply be a different way for them to meet their need to belong or to be in control, or to assert their independence.

As teenagers grow and develop, their needs change. Therefore, it can be useful to be mindful of all their needs and ask if these needs are being met in balance. Sometimes, a need is not only being met, it is being met *too much* – at the expense of meeting other needs, or at the expense of meeting other people's needs – a situation that can have unintended consequences.

EMOTIONAL NEEDS IN BALANCE

As explained in earlier pages, problems with teenagers – and, in fact, with all humans – become manifest when their needs are not being met in balance. When we consider an imbalance, we mostly think of a deficit like a lack of security or control and how this can manifest in unhealthy habits such as increased anxiety, lack of sleep and worry. But, similar to the way in which too much food or alcohol can eventually turn into an obsession or an addiction, this can also happen with regard to our emotional needs. Too much security, attention or control, for example, is not necessarily good for us: it may create an unhealthy expectation that these needs will always be met. It affects a person's ability to develop skills for themselves, and it may cause problems for a teenager in the future. The challenge is to have the emotional needs met in balance.

If you have too much security while you are growing up – if you are mollycoddled and cosseted from the world and from other people – you will find it difficult to develop the tools and resilience required to deal with difficult situations and difficult people. Teenagers who have had everything handed to them on a plate may have no experience of having to work in order to get something they want, such as new clothes or a holiday. They may have no experience of having a summer job or part-time work to earn money for themselves. They may not even know how to clean or cook.

We are doing a great disservice to the next generation by indulging our children in this way: we are not providing them with the skills necessary for them to take care of themselves. They are not learning the important life lesson that reward requires that effort be expended; that clean clothes and a nice meal require an investment of time and energy, and so on. By failing to ensure that they have the requisite life skills, we are not helping them to become autonomous, healthy adults.

Too much security may also result in creating an adult who is either terrified of change or is overly focused on money and success (which for them may represent security). Such a focus can become an obsession, where everything is viewed through the lens of making money or holding on to money, and all interactions and decisions in life are based on weighing up the potential financial gain or loss in each case.

The same imbalance can occur when a person is given too much attention – the little prince or princess who is doted on, and whose every whim is taken seriously. This can sometimes happen if a parent wants to be seen as a 'friend' rather than as a disciplinarian. When children are given too much attention during their formative years, it creates an expectation that they will receive a similar level of attention from everyone they come into contact with in later life. This has the insidious effect of creating the very thing they wish to avoid. Someone who has a greed for attention (i.e. is an attention-seeker), becomes a psychological and emotional drain on others. The more they seek attention, the less they get. Because meeting their need is hugely draining for other people, the attention-seeker is avoided. The attention-seeker's great difficulty is that they can never be satisfied. Their need is so great that the more attention they get, the more they need, thus creating a very unhappy, unfulfilled person. Unfortunately, in Western society we see increasing numbers of such teenagers all around us.

The same is true for the need for control or autonomy. Too much control is not good for either teenagers or adults. We all need a certain amount of choice and control in our lives, but we also get a sense of security from knowing that someone is 'in charge'. By their nature, teenagers are hardwired to push boundaries. While they will rebel and complain whenever reasonable limits are imposed, limits also provide a structure within which they can relax and feel safe.

Giving a teenager too much control can leave them vulnerable to becoming a control freak or a bully, where they *have* to get their own way. Such behaviour sometimes begins at home and then continues as they engage with the outside world. These controlling teenagers may never have been challenged to think of others and consider whether *their* needs were being met. While giving teenagers choice can help them develop a sense of autonomy, the effect of giving teenagers too much control can result in them having a huge sense of entitlement. It's all a question of balance.

When teenagers are very popular – and achieve high recognition, attention, status and control in their social group – the power of this status and control can create a heady mix and leave them vulnerable to misusing this power.

The idealism of the teenage years is wonderful: teenagers are filled with enthusiasm to make a difference, and often have unrealistic dreams and ambitions. They have not yet learned that the world is a hard, tough place that might not live up to their hopes and aspirations. But teenagers' idealism, taken to an extreme, can also cause difficulties. This hunger for a more meaningful life can leave idealistic teenagers vulnerable to unhealthy groups who are purporting to strive for an ideal. Teenagers may not have the experience or the wisdom to discern the manipulation and influence of an unscrupulous group leader who appears to be advocating selfless service to a worthy cause, but who is actually exploiting others.

The consequences of focusing too much on a life of meaning and purpose might be to neglect some of the other emotional needs that nourish us and provide balance and perspective. An unbalanced approach of focusing only on providing service to others can lead to increased stress and, ultimately, to burnout.

Any emotional need, if left unnurtured, or if nurtured too much, can result in a person developing a destructive longing, or an obsession that can cause great problems in the long run.

7

TEENAGERS AND THEIR BRAINS

Now that we have an understanding of what is common to all humans, let us take a look at how teenagers' brains differ from those of the adults and children around them. Science has only recently discovered that the teenage brain is distinctly different from the pre-adolescent brain. Knowing what the key differences are – and what effects these differences can have on behaviour – will help you understand why your adorable pre-teen has changed overnight into a stranger who is now displaying all the hallmarks of a typical moody, monosyllabic and secretive teenager.

The first thing you need to understand is that such changes are quite normal. In fact, if they weren't happening, it would be more worrying. During the teenage years, your child's brain undergoes major changes at the same time as physical changes are also taking place in their body. In particular, during these years, certain hormones trigger the physical changes needed to help them successfully make the transition from child to adult. Simultaneously, neuronal changes in the brain help them create their own identity and become independent.

THE TEENAGE BRAIN – A WORK IN PROGRESS

As we have seen, the brain is a highly dynamic, 'plastic' (i.e. malleable) organ that changes with every new experience. During the teenage years, this is doubly so. Since the late 1990s, brain science has shown why the teenage years are so formative and so significant, and why this is such a challenging period in both a teenager's and a parent's life.

Up until the late 1990s, it was assumed that hormones were responsible for causing behavioural changes in teenagers. But, while hormones are undoubtedly important, they are not the full story. During adolescence, the brain undergoes extensive rewiring. These changes are unique to the adolescent years, and they are quite different to the way the brain develops in childhood. It is these rewiring changes that are responsible for some of the common problems we associate with young people's behaviour during their teenage years.

The brain is an incredibly complex organ and is still relatively poorly understood, even though huge strides have been made in our understanding. Essentially, the brain acts like a control centre that manages the activity of the body. While your genes determine the basic physical structure of the brain, the actual wiring of the brain is determined by your experiences. You are born already programmed to do certain things (such as grasp or suckle). From the moment of birth, the brain begins to build and modify itself, based on what it is learning from the environment. The plasticity of the developing brain allows young people the flexibility to adjust to the demands of their particular environment, thus giving them an increased chance of success in that environment. The acquisition of language is one example of this plasticity. We are all born with the ability to learn any language in the world. However, as the brain is only exposed to certain sounds, by late childhood we lose the ability to pronounce unfamiliar sounds commonly used in foreign languages. The brain allows those parts required for pronunciation of that language to die off, in order to become more efficient and retain only what is deemed essential and no more. The neural networks in the brain respond in a pattern that is established by past experience; the more often a specific pattern is fired in response to a stimulus, the more fixed that pattern becomes. Therefore, a child who is exposed only to the English language will develop strong neural patterns for English, while the patterns for the pronunciation of other language sounds will die away: that is why pronouncing the sounds of new languages is easier the younger we are. Hence the axiom: 'Neurons that fire together wire together.'

Any input that the brain is exposed to shapes the way you experience the next input, and, as stated earlier, *after* you have had a particular experience you are not the same person you were *before* that experience.

Experience colours perception and changes the neural patterns in your brain.

The majority of the neurological changes that take place during the teenage years take place in the frontal lobes. While the frontal lobes are undergoing such changes, the adolescent's ability to make wise choices and deal with temptation is affected. The frontal lobes regulate much of the brain, and the changes that take place there affect overall brain function and promote the development of more complex, subtle thinking. The neurological changes that occur during the teenage years take place at a cellular level. The type of brain cells we are concerned with are called neurons.

Neurons are brain cells that process and transmit information through electrical and chemical signals. There are literally hundreds of billions of neurons in the brain. They connect with other neurons through synapses (the junction point between two neurons) and communicate with each other using chemical messengers. These chemicals influence our brain's processing, along with our behaviour, our thinking and our emotions. When neurons connect to each other they form neural networks.

The brain is also made up of two different types of tissue: grey matter and white matter. Grey matter contains neurons, and white matter is made of axons connecting different parts of grey matter together. Axons are like cables connecting the neuron cell bodies to each other; they are wrapped in a fatty substance called myelin, which gives the tissue a light colour, hence the name 'white matter'.

At approximately age 11 for girls and age 12 for boys, the volume of frontal-lobe grey matter peaks; it then declines throughout adolescence and into young adulthood. This might seem strange, but what actually happens is that up until this point the frontal lobes overgrow and form far more communication points (synapses) than are needed. With the onset of adolescence, the brain then becomes selective and prunes away the synapses that are neither useful nor required. Hundreds of billions of synapses are destroyed during this time. Also, during this pruning process, the synapses that are exercised more through experiences become stronger, whereas the synapses that have been underused are eliminated, thus leading to a reduction in grey matter. As a result, the synapses that form meaningful and useful points of contact are strengthened.

As the amount of grey matter declines, the white matter increases throughout adolescence and into adulthood. The increase in white matter in the brain is due to myelination, where the nerve fibres (axons) of the neurons become wrapped in myelin. Myelin is a substance made of protein and fat, which acts as an insulating layer. This myelination creates an increase in processing speed and faster communication between neurons. This means that neural connections are made quicker, but the neurons have less capacity to change and be flexible. So the adult brain is faster and more efficient, but its ability to change and adapt is less. Myelination serves to strengthen new neural pathways. Adolescence is a time for quick, rapid learning and flexibility, which is then strengthened through myelination for the future.

As a consequence, the neural pathways of activities practised by a teenager will survive and solidify, which highlights the importance of skills learned by teenagers during this developmental period. This process works wonderfully when teenagers are learning new, useful skills, e.g. driving. But it is not so useful if an adolescent experiences a great deal of pain and trauma during their teenage years, or if what they learn is unhelpful or destructive behaviour.

The decline in grey-matter volume in teenage brains does not mean that the frontal lobes are not working hard. In fact, it seems that as you mature you rely more on the frontal lobes to organise and control behaviour. As the volume of grey matter decreases, the frontal-lobe-dependent tasks (such as problem-solving and planning) become more focused, accurate and efficient. This maturation ensures that people adapt to their environment and embed cultural norms and life experiences in their neural pathways. As a result, adolescents naturally get better at doing the kind of things that the frontal lobes control, such as making good decisions about the future and controlling impulses. Until the maturation process is complete, however, adolescents will continue to make unwise, immature decisions. It takes time and maturity to develop the ability to stop and reflect, to predict consequences and to make forward-thinking decisions.

These changes in the brain not only help teenagers to develop social skills and the ability to solve complex problems, but to also have the mental flexibility needed to learn new skills. Ultimately, it is the natural changes in brain wiring – and not simply hormones – that make adolescence such a distinct period of development. As adolescents move away from parents, as well as trying out different identities and exploring the world more, their brains absorb all these new experiences while simultaneously soaking up a great deal of information.

TEENAGERS AND HORMONES

In addition to the pruning and myelination changes occurring in the teenager's brain, their body is also undergoing many hormonal changes, which affect their emotional state and mood. This may go some way to explain why within a short period of time teenagers can go from being the very personification of sweetness and light to being grumpy and monosyllabic.

The hormonal changes they are undergoing will depend on the sex of your teenager, as they are different in boys and girls. Your child's sex is determined at conception, and the genes the child has inherited will also determine many of his or her physical characteristics. In addition, genes determine the changes that happen to your child in the womb, as well as in early childhood and in both the pre-adolescent and teenage years. The hormones that determine the sex of a child have a direct impact on the development of the child's brain. So, depending on whether your child is a boy or a girl, their brains will develop differently and at different rates.

For example, when they are born, male babies are less developmentally mature, more emotionally sensitive and, consequently, more dependent. Female babies, on the other hand, are in general, more resilient and are born more developmentally mature and self-reliant. Up until recently, these differences were often put down to environmental factors and how the two sexes were treated. Now, however, it is generally accepted by scientists that these differences are caused by sex-specific distinctions.

These findings are generalities and obviously do not apply to all girls and boys. Each person is unique and has abilities and talents in many areas, but a definite trend in abilities has been acknowledged in the research. Some of these differences are apparent early in life.

When a child reaches the teenage years, nature knows that it is now time to enhance these differences, in order to help them survive in the adult world. Thus, male and female hormones kick in automatically.

The Teenage Boy's Brain

The hormone that triggers changes in the teenage boy's brain is testosterone, which dramatically increases between the ages of 10 and 15. His brain is now being flooded with twenty times the level of testosterone he has had up to this point, and this results in creating new thoughts and behaviours, as well as creating changes in his body. Just as testosterone activates the growth of his muscles and bones, and deepens his voice and makes his pubic hair grow, it also makes the sexual circuits in the brain's hypothalamus grow more than twice as large as those in a girl's brain. His brain is now constructed to emphasise sexual pursuit and bring it to the forefront of his mind. This can be disturbing to a boy in early puberty as he gets used to his preoccupation with sex – something that can appear to control him. The other hormone that comes into play at this time is vasopressin, which, together with testosterone, makes the young teenage boy territorial and increasingly sensitive about his peers' perception of him. He becomes sensitive to their jeers and putdowns – whether they are real or imagined.

When testosterone and vasopressin are combined with the stress hormone cortisol, the teenager's body becomes supercharged in its reaction to challenges, such as his need for status within his peer group. Not every boy will want to be at the top of his hierarchical peer group, but he will certainly not want to be at the bottom, and this can mean that boys are more vulnerable to seeking status through taking risks, something that often lands them in trouble.

It takes approximately eight or nine years for these hormonal changes to cease and for the boy's enhanced brain to stabilise. This process does not conclude until he is in his mid- to late twenties. It is important for frustrated parents to remember that teenage boys are not trying to be difficult; the fact is that at this stage in their young lives their brains are not hardwired to give much thought to the future. A teenage boy's brain is so controlled by the testosterone and vasopressin activating his sex and aggression circuits that it is very difficult for him for focus on his studies. He will constantly be drawn to the sight of someone in his class whom he fancies, or to some other boy in his class who is teasing him and distracting him. As he tries to regain focus, his hormones will take control and his homework will be put on the back burner. On top of that, we need to factor in the pressure of social media in all its guises – high-tech distractions (particularly when someone he fancies is online) – as well as various sports and games that may be constantly demanding his attention. Therefore, in general, getting boys to do homework will tend to be a greater battle than getting teenage girls to knuckle down.

Everything about the school system is in conflict with a teenage boy's brain. He is seeking adventure and risk and the school is seeking order and control. The school system is, furthermore, completely at odds with his newly developed sleep pattern (see Chapter 12). During the teenage years, the sleep patterns of both sexes change, but boys' patterns change more so than those of girls. We shouldn't be surprised therefore that boys cause most of the disruption in school and that, across the world, more boys than girls drop out of school permanently.

The Teenage Girl's Brain

The hormones that trigger changes in an adolescent girl are oestrogen and progesterone. Nature is preparing her to enter the adult world of women and therefore usually from the age of 10 onwards she will begin to experience the oestrogen and progesterone surges that are produced in monthly waves.

Many parts of the female brain are particularly sensitive to oestrogen and progesterone. For example, the hippocampus is important for memory and learning, and the amygdala (the part of the brain that monitors the environment for threats) can prompt the production of the stress hormone cortisol. These three hormones ensure that a teenage girl becomes more sensitive to emotional nuances of approval and disapproval, acceptance and rejection. She becomes overly sensitive to others and the changes in her body may bring about new-found sexual attention, which may be very confusing for her.

Around this time, girls begin to react more to relationship stresses, while boys seem to be more sensitive to challenges to their status. The fluctuation of hormones throughout a girl's monthly cycle adds another dimension to her irrational responses. During the first two weeks of her cycle, when oestrogen is high, a girl is more likely to be relaxed and socially outgoing. During the last two weeks of her cycle, however, when the level of progesterone is high and the level of oestrogen is lower (see Figure 3), she will probably be more sensitive and irritable, and will want to be on her own.

Figure 3: Oestrogen–Progesterone Cycles

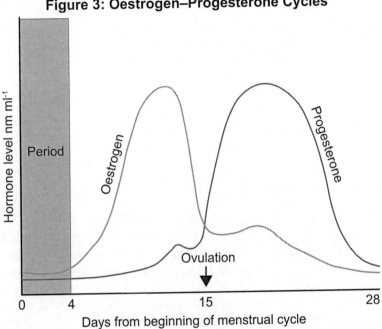

The fluctuations of oestrogen and progesterone begin to influence her in many ways. She begins to think and feel differently, perhaps focusing on how she looks. She also begins to act differently as age-old genetic blueprints are directing her with instructions to focus on her body and her place in her group. She begins to measure herself against her peers and media images of attractive females and she becomes acutely aware of male attention.

Oestrogen acts like a fuel rushing through her brain, concentrating her on her appearance, and she will spend hours ruminating on whether boys find her attractive. Throughout history, girls have always focused on whether or not boys considered them attractive. This is driven by two intertwining factors: first, girls' hormones create a perception in their brains that this is the most important thing at this point in their lives and, second, society and the media can often place the same emphasis on the importance of a girl's physical appearance. These two factors working together can lead your teenage daughter to obsess about her weight, her breast size or other physical attributes. A teenage girl will act out some version of this behaviour irrespective of the strength of the media's influence on her self-image.

But they are not only focused on boys; friendships with other girls also become intensely important. They are driven by a desire to connect, as in prehistoric times her survival would have very much depended on being part of a group. Girls are hardwired to create strong friendships with other females; it helps lower their stress and activates the pleasurable hormone oxytocin. This is why girls are motivated to seek out relationships and why they get so much pleasure from talking and connecting with other females.

Knowledge of these age-old drives in both boys and girls – combined with knowledge of the nature of the hormones fuelling these drives – can help parents to understand their sons and daughters, and it can help to steer them safely through these turbulent teenage years.

8

TEENAGERS AND RISK

The 'reward system' within the brain has the potential to inadvertently cause great difficulties in all of us – adults and teenagers alike. The reward system is an intrinsic part of our makeup. Just like all living creatures, we are biologically primed to avoid what causes us pain and to seek out what gives us pleasure. All living beings have some kind of reward system that controls this instinctive response. So, if teenagers do something that activates their reward system – something that gives them pleasure – it is likely that they will behave that way again. This holds true no matter what the particular reward is – a smile, a chocolate bar, a drink, a goal in football or an A+ in an end-of-term exam.

THE 'REWARD SYSTEM'

As explained in Chapter 2, every human being has both physical and emotional needs. When these needs are met, we experience pleasure to some degree. The physical needs of eating, drinking, sleeping, exercise, etc. are all associated with pleasure. Indeed, this is nature's way of ensuring that we continue to repeat a behaviour that is critical for our survival. The same principle holds true for emotional needs: when these needs are met we also experience a feeling of pleasure. For example, consider for a moment how you feel after you have spent time chatting with a close friend, or after you have achieved a goal or completed a task: these are all accompanied by a feeling of pleasure. You are being rewarded for doing something that meets your needs in some way, and this ensures that you continue with that behaviour.

In order to ensure the survival and evolution of humans, it was necessary that we developed to be flexible, adaptable and curious. Without this we would not have survived in a constantly changing environment. So we feel pleasure whenever we experience something new, or discover something new about the world – we are being rewarded for growing and learning and the pleasure we experience ensures that we don't stagnate. Pleasure is like nature's 'carrot', and it is used to encourage us to continue to grow and learn, and to be creative and flexible.

So, How Does This Work?

So we see that learning and discovering is pleasurable. Think back to times in your own life when you acquired a new skill – mastered riding a bike, learned to speak French, solved a difficult mathematical problem. Maybe you baked a cake for the first time, grew plants from seed or painted a picture. Think back to the feeling of satisfaction you got the first time you achieved something new. That feeling of pleasure is nature's way of ensuring we are all motivated to try out new things, so that we develop and grow. This aids our survival as we create more effective and efficient ways to get our needs met.

In order to ensure that we continue growing and learning, we first get an initial burst of pleasure but each time we repeat the task or behaviour, the pleasure is gradually reduced. As we continue to repeat it the pleasure continues to reduce until it becomes incorporated as a normal part of our everyday life. You do not experience the same degree of pleasure today when you drive to the supermarket as you did the first day you managed to drive a car on your own, or the first time you stood on a surfboard or painted a picture. Nature lessens the pleasure accordingly as the activity becomes more normal and everyday.

The high degree of pleasure only comes when we experience something new, so this means that our biological systems are designed to drive us to keep looking for new ways to meet our needs, and to continue to stretch and challenge ourselves. This process is called the reward system, and it is the same system that in teenagers can positively motivate them to stretch themselves to achieve, or, conversely, to destructively trap themselves in an endless search for pleasure. Crucially, the reward system is what is hijacked when a person becomes addicted (see Chapter 20).

The reward system is controlled by the motivational hormone dopamine. Dopamine works by signalling to the brain that something important has just happened and that the brain should pay attention or *do something* and learn from it. Dopamine is a motivator. The pleasure is caused by endorphins, chemicals akin to opiates. In fact, just remembering the pleasure can be enough to motivate us to repeat whatever behaviour generated the pleasure in the first place.

During adolescence, the dopamine reward system is very excitable and hyperactive. It motivates youngsters to seek out activities or to engage in behaviours that they expect will bring them pleasure. Crucially, the reward system is activated not only by the reward itself, but also by the *expectation of a reward*. Sometimes, the expectation can be a more powerful motivator than the reward itself as it creates a strong belief that certain behaviours will deliver the same degree of pleasure yet again.

As a consequence, this hyperactive reward system can lead us to repeat mindless or destructive activities that were associated with pleasure in the past. In the case of teenage boys, a risky stunt or a practical joke might be repeated because it once increased his status with his peer group, triggering a dopamine rush in his brain. We now know that the brain's receptivity to dopamine is at its highest during adolescence – far higher than in children or adults. This perhaps explains why adolescents are so susceptible to risk-taking and seem to have no concept of consequences. Quite simply, they are blinded by the thrill and expectation of pleasure.

Perhaps we can better appreciate the great appeal to adolescents of risk-taking when we understand that new experiences and learning bring them the highest degree of pleasure.

These changes in the hyperactivity of the reward system make substance abuse and drug dependence much more likely during adolescence. It is therefore easy to see how a hyperactive reward system response (especially when combined with the effect of immature frontal lobes, which help you to consider consequences) can lead to a range of high-risk behaviours in teenagers. Add to this vulnerable scenario the effect of oxytocin – the hormone that bonds you to others and makes social connections more rewarding. The teenage brain is more sensitive to oxytocin, similar to the way it is sensitive to dopamine. In the teenage brain, the neural networks of reward and social connection overlap and engage each other; this is the reason why teenagers prefer the company of their peers. Their peers provide more novelty than either their parents or their siblings, therefore peer pressure becomes a particularly strong motivator during the teenage years. The teenager's need to be accepted as part of the group, and to have status within that group, takes on additional prominence.

Research carried out by Dustin Albert and Laurence Steinberg at Temple University in the US has shown that adults and teenagers respond differently when performing in front of their friends. For example, when adults and teenagers were observed playing a simple video driving game, the researchers showed that the teenagers took more risks than the adults. But the number of risks taken increased yet again when the teenagers' friends were in the room and they were being observed by them. This illustrates just how susceptible teenagers are to projecting a certain image to their friends. Why should a teenager take more risks just because a friend is watching? The study showed that the teenagers' reward system *was more active* when they took a risk in front of their friends. It proved that the thrill of the risk, coupled with the approval of the friends, was a heady combination and highly rewarding.

This finding helps to explain why teenagers are five times more likely to be involved in car crashes when friends are in the car, and why they are more likely to commit crimes when they are in groups. It also explains why some teenagers who seem to be very responsible in some situations (such as when they are at school or at home) can behave really irresponsibly when they are with their peers. Taking risks *feels good* for teens.

Dopamine stimulates the frontal lobes of the brain to pay attention, to focus on some specific, immediate action, and to ignore other considerations. But remember, the frontal lobes of a teenager lack maturity and their ability to delay gratification is immature and underdeveloped. We know from research that teenagers are more likely to choose immediate, small rewards, and to reject large rewards in the future. Adults, for the most part, have mastered this ability, and it seems logical to them to wait for a larger reward. Teenagers, unfortunately, have not, and so they are lured by the thrill they get from instant gratification.

How Risk-Taking Helps

Some of the behaviour that is synonymous with teenagers is also thought to have a biological basis. We have seen how dopamine affects the developing brain and how it pushes adolescents to explore the world outside their home and discover things for themselves. This push to the outside world facilitates the process of developing a sense of their own identity. It is only by going out and exploring the world that any individual can develop their own judgements and opinions, based on their own experiences, instead of merely emulating their parents' viewpoints. The experience gained gives them the opportunity to develop their own values and become independent people in their own right.

Risk-taking is much stronger in adolescence (when the brain is pruning away neural pathways that are no longer required) than it is in childhood (when the brain is growing). The predisposition to risk-taking is due to the fact that during this 'pruning time' the brain is becoming more discriminatory; it is discarding those areas that are no longer useful, and growing areas that are being used and developed. Risk-taking facilitates this learning and discrimination by determining what works and what doesn't work so well in the world. The brain is being moulded through selection and pruning. Risk-taking facilitates learning for oneself. Risk also helps teenagers interact with and earn the respect of their peers, and this helps to build teenagers' confidence and independence. It explains why the activities that adolescents experience during these years are both a marvellous opportunity for neurological and psychological growth and a very risky time – not least because in the majority of cases teenagers do not have the maturity and the capacity to understand the risks they are taking.

Scientists believe that the rebellion that is typical of this phase is driven by a natural biological urge and is not a conscious choice. This drive is evolutionary in origin and it derives from the instinct to reproduce, which is inherent in all animals. The need to get away from our families and hook up with new groups is nature's way of ensuring that we do not reproduce with others in our gene pool. So, when your teenager announces that they cannot stand being in your home and much prefer the house of a friend down the road, remember that this behaviour is the result of a biological drive to ensure they mix with new people. In addition, when they express the desire to move to another city or country because 'it's so boring/uncool around here', try to resist the natural response to feel hurt and rejected. Remember that, yet again, this is nature's way of ensuring healthy offspring by drawing from a different gene pool; that it is a necessary urge in the context of the biological consequences of mating too closely with your own gene pool. As they mature into their twenties and thirties, your children will learn to appreciate the positives of their families and their roots, and may surprise you with accounts of how much they miss their family and home.

The parent–child separation process – and the inevitable conflict that accompanies it – is normal and, if handled properly, is perfectly healthy. While this has been the case for millennia, today's road to independence can be stressful and confusing, given the staggering array of opportunities and pitfalls awaiting teenagers in a fast-paced world. Try to keep a positive view of your teenager in mind when you are at your wits' end. Remember that with each passing day their brain is developing and growing. It is getting better at assessing the consequences of risk, understanding the positive and negative effects of rebellion, and learning how to choose battles appropriately. Your teenager is also getting better at delaying gratification, thinking about the future and the consequences of today's actions.

Without risk-taking and rebellion, the transition from childhood to adulthood would be severely hampered. The rebellion and risks taken – and the lessons learned as a result – propel the adolescent from dependence to independence. They force the teenager out of the security of their family and into the world, and they then learn to stand on their own two feet. Imagine what would happen if they didn't. They might never leave home at all!

Part III

LIVING WITH TEENAGERS

9

TEENAGERS AND COMMUNICATION

Parents often ask the question: 'How do you communicate with teenagers, given that they can be moody, withdrawn, sullen, uncommunicative, angry, anxious or confused?' Often, teenagers haven't mastered basic communication skills and by the time they reach their mid- to late teens their methods of communication may leave a lot to be desired. Their moodiness and angry outbursts can irritate even the most patient and tolerant of parents. How can you learn to communicate with each other in a way that is effective for both, while simultaneously keeping family life as calm as possible?

The most important thing that you need to keep at the forefront of your mind when dealing with teenagers is to manage your own emotions and reactions. If you don't, what you regard as an innocuous conversation may quickly escalate into a row, culminating in hurt feelings and regrets on both sides. Remember, the onus is always on you, the adult, to show a good example. Hopefully, your brain has matured sufficiently to enable you to manage your own emotions. Difficult as it may be, when communicating with your teenage son or daughter you need to behave in the same way as you did when they were an anxious or angry toddler. In other words, stand back from their emotional outbursts, try to see the situation as they see it, and then respond appropriately.

The fact is, more than ten years after your teenager went through the 'terrible twos', you are now likely to be faced with similar tantrums – the only difference being that your son or daughter now looks grown up and may be taller than you. Indeed, while teenagers may frequently remind us of how grown up they are, they are anything but. When they feel emotional, they may be quite unable to calm down their emotional brain. For this reason, you need to cut them some slack.

The following tips should prove useful when you are communicating with teenagers and will help improve your relationship with them (note: they apply equally to both boys and girls):

1. *Be genuinely interested in them.* Get to know who they are, what they like, who they hang out with, what music they listen to and who their friends are. As with adults, it is invariably easier to have a conversation with someone if you can talk to them about things that are important in their world. Having a 'hook' for the conversation means you can avoid those general, open-ended questions that all teenagers hate, such as 'How was school today?' Instead, ask them about something specific – the match, the French class, their friends Peter and Melissa.

2. *Give them your full attention.* Look at them when you are talking to them and use non-verbal signs of interest, such as nodding, or appropriate facial expressions and verbal responses that encourage them to keep talking.

3. *Invite their friends around for supper or to watch a film.* It really helps if you actually know or have met the people they hang around with.

4. *Where possible, try to see things from their perspective.* Try to step into their shoes and imagine how their emotional needs are being met. Also how their emotions are colouring their thinking on a given situation or topic.

5. *Make it as easy as possible for them to approach you with any concerns they may have.* This is really important. If they feel they can come to you when they are confused, concerned or in trouble, you will be a rock for them. It is therefore absolutely essential that you keep the lines of communication open between you as much as possible.

TALKING TO TEENAGE BOYS

If your teenager is a boy, he will be less likely to sit down with you and have a heart-to-heart conversation the way a girl might do. If you want to get him to talk, the best way to do this is to engage in some activity together. Boys will generally open up more when they are distracted by activities such as making a meal, painting an area of the house, tidying the garden, clearing out the garage, and so on. Chatting to your teenage son while you engage in these activities will serve to draw him out and, as a consequence, you are more likely to hear about what is going on in his life.

Having a conversation while driving somewhere also works well. If he is in the passenger seat, watching the city or countryside go by, you have a much better chance of getting your teenage son to open up. Most boys find sitting down face-to-face for a conversation with a parent intimidating; it makes them feel they are being interrogated, and so they tend to clam up. So, come up with an excuse to drive him somewhere that is a distance from your home – say at least an hour away – and you may be surprised by what you will find out. Alternatively, drive him and his friends to a concert or a sports event. By just listening to their conversation you will be able to glean quite a bit about his place in the group, how he fits in and what issues are preoccupying him.

If the two of you are alone together and engaged in some activity, give him plenty of time to respond to your questions. Generally, boys take much longer than girls to gather their thoughts before answering a question. Indeed, they may appear to have finished talking when in reality they are just gathering their thoughts for the next thing they will say. This is particularly so if the topic is an emotional one for them. Consequently, don't jump in too soon with your comments or follow-up questions. If you do, he will feel you are not taking him seriously and you will end up with monosyllabic answers. Another important point to remember is that boys tend to speak in shorter sentences. So, it will help if you match his style of speaking. Say what you need to say concisely. Then stop and give him a chance to respond.

Ask his opinion. Say: 'How would you go about X?' or 'What do you think about Y?' Asking for his opinion is a much better way to get him talking than asking him questions, which can feel like an interrogation. Asking for his opinion shows that you respect his judgement. More-over, it will create a better opportunity for the two of you to have a real conversation.

If you must ask him questions, make sure they are straightforward ones such as 'What part of Maths do you find most difficult?', 'Did Peter go to the match?' or 'What was the score?' These types of questions will be easier for him to answer – much easier than the emotionally laden 'How did you feel about that?' You can broach the subject of how he is feeling later, when he has opened up a bit.

Notice his moods and just acknowledge them to him. He may not want to talk about his mood, or what is bothering him, but knowing that you have noticed will make a difference to him. A comment such as 'You're in great form today' or 'You look a bit down, are you okay?' will be appreciated, even if he doesn't indicate this to you at the time. And don't be put off if you don't get a response. The absence of a response does not mean your comment has not been noted.

TALKING TO TEENAGE GIRLS

As with boys, a teenage girl needs to build a relationship of trust. She needs to know that you care, and this does not happen overnight. It takes time. While some teenage girls can be very good at hiding their feelings, most are extremely emotional. Fluctuations in their hormonal levels invariably have an effect on their mood and, as a result, they may feel 'all over the place', which can be very unsettling and upsetting for a girl who, up to now, may have felt quite stable.

Your role is to be steady for your teenage daughter as she navigates the rollercoaster of her menstrual cycle and how it affects her emotions, sleep patterns and stress levels. In order to build a relationship with her, you need to spend quality time getting involved in activities that she is interested in. This will allow her to relax, and it will help build closeness and trust between you. The main thing, as with boys, is to *listen*. Resist, as much as you can, the temptation to judge her or lose patience with her, particularly if she has unrealistic plans or ideas, or if she disagrees with you.

Remember, this is a time when she is learning for herself, and her sense of herself and her confidence can be easily dinted by thoughtless or hurtful remarks. Listening shows her you understand that she needs to talk about something she may be concerned about, or needs some advice on. Listen, take your time, and try not to jump in too quickly. Ask her what *she* thinks and what ideas *she* has. Help her to think through her ideas and to anticipate the possible consequences and repercussion of different actions. You can do this by asking her what she thinks might happen if she took a particular approach or action.

It is useful to share experiences with her, so if she likes reading, try reading the books she is interested in and share the experience. Or go to the cinema together, listen to the music she likes, show an interest in what is happening in her life and ask her for her opinion on current events.

Above all, try to resist becoming impatient with her if she has immature ideas. Losing your temper with her or making denigrating remarks about her could be remembered by her for a long time to come. Losing control over your own emotions and lashing out at a teenager will only damage any trust you have built up between you.

How to Talk to Emotional Teenagers

The Open-Loop System

All of us – adults and teenagers alike – are unconsciously affected by, and acutely aware of, the moods and humours of those around us. The reason why we are affected is due to what is called the 'open loop' nature of the brain's limbic system or emotional brain. This open-loop system allows you to pick up or transmit emotional states to or from others.

People have always instinctively known that we pick up on someone's angry mood, their envy or even their fear, and that it can affect us. Now, however, scientists are able to observe it in practice, using modern brain-imaging technology. If people are in close contact with one another, they will inevitably be 'infected' by the emotions of those around them (you pick up the emotional 'vibes'). Being mindful of your own emotional state and being aware that you can possibly 'pick up' anger and frustration from your teenager can help you to stay steady and calm, while, hopefully, at the same time aiming to transmit calmness to them.

So, start with yourself. Make sure that you manage your own stress levels. Take time out, and learn to relax. And before you initiate a conversation with your teenager, make sure that you actually have the time and the head space to listen to – and take on board – what is going on in their world.

Outlined below are some practical approaches to managing the parent–teenager conversation process, and creating a useful and positive outcome for both of you. It is known as RIGAAR (developed by Joe Griffin and Ivan Tyrrell of the Human Givens College) and it works as follows:

R = Rapport-building
I = Information-gathering
G = Goal-setting
A = Accessing resources
A = Agreeing a strategy
R = Rehearse

Step One: Rapport-Building

In order to communicate effectively, you have to give your teenager some exclusive attention, which can be difficult to do in a busy household. You need to choose the time and the place carefully, so that you are not rushed or stressed. If you are under pressure, it is a good idea to let them know that you realise they are upset, and arrange to talk to them when it is more convenient.

When you are talking to your teenager, give them your full attention. Make it clear that you are interested in what is going on in their lives – or in whatever is upsetting them – by mirroring their body language, tone of voice and vocabulary. So, for example, if they are standing and you are sitting, either suggest that they sit down, or simply stand up while talking to them. If they are speaking loudly, speak almost as loudly as them. This conveys non-verbally that you empathise with their emotional state.

The following is an example of two scenarios where Jack (aged 13) comes home from school. In Scenario 1, the conversation goes like this:

Jack: 'Mr Doyle is a prat! You wouldn't believe what he said to me today.'
You could respond: 'Oh come on! Mr Doyle is a really good teacher. What did you do to annoy him?'

This immediately gives Jack the idea that you are on Mr Doyle's side, and that you don't understand his point of view.

But, in Scenario 2, you could respond something along the following lines:

> 'Oh dear. Listen Jack, I can see you are really upset about what Mr Doyle said. Why don't we sit down when I have fed the others and you can tell me all about it?'

As this is an emotional subject for Jack, and as he really wants to talk about it right now, he is likely to say something along the lines of:

> 'Oh it doesn't matter. ... Forget it!'

You could reply with:

> 'But Jack, it does matter. I really want to know what happened. But I can't give it the attention it deserves right now. Why don't you make a start on your homework, and I'll come up to your room when I've got things sorted here?'

In this second scenario, you are acknowledging the importance of his experience and letting him know that you really do care about how he feels, irrespective of whether what Mr Doyle said to him was justified or not.

Step Two: Information-Gathering and Listening

A good model for communicating with anyone – and especially teenagers – is to first try to understand their viewpoint; to listen, no matter how unreasonable or daft that viewpoint might seem to you. This is sometimes referred to as 'entering their model of reality'. At this point, simply listen, without interrupting, giving advice or asking questions. The teenager can be prompted to continue if you interject every so often with comments such as 'Yes', 'Go on', 'I see' and 'I know what you mean'.

It is a good idea to repeat back a summary of what you have heard, as this reassures them that you have been listening carefully. Also, it gives them an opportunity to clarify any misunderstandings. It is also useful to put a name on what it is that you sense they are feeling, as this can serve to help them organise their own thoughts and calm themselves down. The following is an example of how this might be done:

> **Parent:** 'Gosh Jack, it seems to me that you are very frustrated with Mr Doyle, as no matter how hard you try he criticises your homework.'
>
> **Jack:** 'Yeah, and he never says a word to Sam or Pete. And they don't do even a fraction of the research and homework that I do.'
>
> **Parent:** 'That sounds really frustrating alright!'

Reframe the Problem in a Different Light

This is a very powerful technique that can help a teenager change the meaning of something that has happened. The 'frame' that we put on an experience is the meaning that we associate with it. To reframe it means to put a different frame or interpretation on what has occurred.

When we get emotional, we can stay locked in a negative interpretation and find it difficult to step back and see things from a different angle that may be more useful and accurate. In the case of the above example, you could reframe Jack's interaction with Mr Doyle by suggesting that teachers only bother to criticise the work of the students they believe have real potential. This reframes the situation for Jack and shows him that Mr Doyle's criticism was, in fact, a statement of belief in Jack's ability. Following this line of reasoning could really serve to motivate Jack, as opposed to catapulting him into a demotivated state.

The 'reframe' dialogue might now continue as follows:

> **Parent:** 'So, Mr Doyle obviously believes that you have the potential to get an A, whereas maybe he doesn't see that with every student.'

Changing the frame can make all the difference. The following are some additional reframes you might find useful:

> **Parent:** 'I can see that you're feeling very frustrated at the moment.'
>
> *or* **Parent:** 'So, you haven't figured out what he's looking for in an essay yet.'

or **Jack:** 'It always happens to me.'
Parent: 'It was just bad luck. You were in the wrong place at the wrong time.'

As these examples illustrate, listening to the problem, and then summarising and reframing it, can make all the difference to a teenager – or to anyone else you are communicating with for that matter. Reframing helps us to see things from a different point of view; it opens up the possibility of solutions and provides us with an exit route from our 'blocked' emotional standpoint.

Step Three: Goal-Setting

It is important to clearly state and repeat back what you believe your teenager wants or needs, so that you can both agree on what is causing their upset.

> **Parent:** 'So, you really want to get an A from Mr Doyle?'

By asking the question, it shows that you want to understand what is upsetting him, and if you have misunderstood it can be clarified. For example, Jack might be merely upset about how he was spoken to by Mr Doyle, and is not all that bothered about getting an A.

Clarifying and summarising is important because misunderstandings can arise between parents and teenagers about the reasons that lie behind the teenager's upset. Based on their adult viewpoint, the parent may inadvertently make certain assumptions, whereas the teenager may have a completely different perspective on the issue.

Step Four: Accessing Resources – Remind Them of Their Strengths

If you are dealing with a teenager who is experiencing disappointment or rejection, it is a good idea to build up hope of finding a solution by reminding them of all they have going for them. There is a caveat, however, and it is this: whatever examples you cite need to be authentic. Teenagers are just as good as adults at sniffing out disingenuous comments and praise. Whatever you say has to be credible in the context of the individual you are talking to.

Think of recent successes in any area of their lives. If they display determination and resilience in sport, for example, refer to that. Remind them that if they have resilience in one area of their lives, they then just need to transfer that resilience to other areas. Alternatively, remind them of positive things that other people have said about them – such as their teachers, siblings, friends, family members, coaches or mentors. If sporting success is not relevant, look to other areas of their lives such as their hobbies, interests, friendships or talents. Remind them that they are determined, loyal, courageous, creative, funny, kind, caring – or whatever adjective fits your teenager. For example, you might say something like the following:

'Jack, I know you have great determination when you put your mind to something. Look at how you trained to get on the football team. You never missed a training session, and all that effort paid off in the end. You are a very determined young man.'

Again, you need to be sensitive here. Whatever you say must be genuine, and it must have a resonance for your teenager. If the praise is superficial and unfounded, it will fall flat. Conversely, praise that is authentic will help to build their self-esteem.

Step Five: Agreeing a Strategy

It is only when a teenager has calmed down somewhat that you can begin to look for solutions together. Giving advice or coming up with answers before this point (when they are still emotional) will only serve to increase their emotional level. They will simply become resistant to whatever suggestions and advice you have to offer. First and foremost they need to feel heard, feel that you understand their point of view and are on their side: only then will they be calm enough to envisage possible solutions. Jumping to this stage too early will merely cause friction.

Sometimes, if you manage to successfully reframe the problem for a teenager, they themselves will come up with their own solutions. For example, with regard to the confrontation with Mr Doyle, Jack might now tell you:

'Melanie manages to get an A every time. Maybe I could read her essays and get some ideas on what she does.'

When a teenager comes up with a solution themselves, they are much more likely to follow it through than if the suggestion came from a parent. Encouraging them to come up with their own solutions is always far more beneficial in the long run. To do this, you might ask:

'So, what do you think you could do that might help you get better marks?'

By asking the teenager to come up with a solution, you are encouraging them to make the shift from their emotional brain to their thinking (i.e. rational) brain. You might also ask:

'What has worked in the past when dealing with Mr Doyle?'
or 'How do the other people in your class deal with Mr Doyle?'

By doing this, you are asking your teenager to draw on their memory to figure out what worked in the past. For example, you might say:

'Imagine you got an A from Mr Doyle. What do you think you would have done differently to get the A?'
or 'What have you done differently when you got an A from other teachers?'

You are asking your teenager to think rather than emote. You are asking them to imagine positive changes by using the phrase 'you got an A' rather than 'if you got an A', and this creates hope.

Offering Suggestions

If you decide to offer suggestions, do so cautiously and remember that if you have faith in your teenager, they will learn to have more confidence in themselves. If you are constantly getting 'I dunno' responses to the questions you ask your teenager, a useful thing to do is to give some advice but wrapped up in a story so that it doesn't appear as if you are doing so. For example, perhaps you know the solution to the problem of Jack not getting an A. Maybe Mr Doyle has made it clear to you that Jack's ideas are very good but his homework is too rushed or incomplete. Saying this directly to Jack would only make him defensive, so saying it indirectly may be much more effective. It might go something along the following lines:

> 'When I was in school, my friend Denise was really good at English essays. The night it was given out as homework, she used to get her ideas down on paper and do a very rough draft. Then, a few days later, when her mind was clearer, she would pick it up again and she would redo the essay from scratch using her original rough draft as reference. That always worked really well for her.'

At this point, it is important to change the subject. You have planted a seed. Now let it germinate. To create a suitable distraction, suggest you both have a cup of tea, or take a break and talk about something else for a while. It would be a good time to remind your teenager about all their good points and the resources they have to draw on:

> 'Anyway, let's go downstairs and have a cuppa. I'm sure you'll figure it out. You're very determined and really good at problem-solving. I know you can do anything you focus your mind on.'

Step Six: Rehearse Success

Now engage your teenager's imagination. See if they can visualise what they are going to do in the future. You might ask questions such as:

> 'Can you see yourself getting help from Melanie?'
> or 'How do you think Mr Doyle will respond to your request for help?'

This helps them weigh up their solution to see how it fits for them. Jack may find that he couldn't imagine himself asking Melanie for help, so that is not going to work. Or he may find that he can. This solution feels right and he can imagine himself carrying it out.

It can even help to talk about the power of the imagination and how visualisation is commonly used by sports psychologists. (This would be especially effective for teenagers who are involved in sport.) Let them know that using their imagination is a very natural – and very powerful – thing to do. Remind them of times they used to daydream about being another character, or achieving a particular ambition. Say something like:

> 'Using your imagination is like rehearsing a play. The more you rehearse, the more you improve your performance.'

Explain that what is genuinely useless is visualising failure. If they visualise failure, all they are actually doing is using their imagination to rehearse what they don't want to happen. You could lighten up the conversation a bit and get them to see the funny side of their current predicament, ask them to imagine the drama group at school rehearsing everything they didn't want to happen on stage on the night of a production. The careful use of humour can be one of the quickest and simplest ways to reframe a problem and create a good mood.

WHEN THEY SCREW UP

Young people can be very resistant to talking about their problems and it is really important not to blame or shame them. Blame or shame can have a silencing and paralysing effect on anyone and as a result they may completely clam up and refuse to speak about the problem. If they see the problem as an integral part of themselves, they will find it very hard to see a way out of their situation.

Helping them to access their 'observing self' (see page 24) will allow them separate themselves from the problem. The more emotional they are, the more difficult this will be, so do what you can to help them calm down initially. By getting them into their observing self you can help them to see that they are separate from the problem, and it is not an integral part of themselves. They can see their difficulties from the outside, and it reduces any feelings of shame or blame that they may have been piling on themselves. Seeing the difficulty from a different point of view can help them reflect on it. When blame and shame are reduced, they are in a better position to access their own creativity and inventiveness, which may help them to come up with their own solutions.

When we take blame out of the picture it can really open up the conversation and reduce the number of 'I dunno' responses. It can be creative and playful. You could start by giving the problem a name. Call it 'Distraction' or 'Temper' or 'Envy'. You could ask questions that assume that the problem is external to them, such as:

'When Distraction appears, what brings it on?'
or 'When did you first notice that you were being bothered by Envy?'

If the problem is anger, speak about it as if it were a separate entity with a mind of its own:

'It looks like Temper is not around right now. What is it like when it's gone?'

Separating them from the problem helps the young person to see ways of overcoming the problem behaviour and emphasises their ability to do so.

'You are not your temper. I'm sure you can find a way to take control of it and stay calm.'

Emphasise the young person's power to overcome the difficulty by saying:

'When Anxiety appears, what is the most helpful thing you can do to calm it down?'

While it is important not to blame or shame a teenager, don't be too concerned if they are feeling guilty or ashamed of themselves. Remember, a healthy dose of guilt is not necessarily a bad thing. It is normal to feel guilty if you have done something cruel or nasty. Guilt serves to stop us repeating destructive behaviour in the future.

A Final Word of Warning When Communicating with Teenagers

Keep a watchful eye out for your own envy creeping in and taking you by surprise. It can happen at any age, but being confronted by an attractive young man or woman who is setting out on life's journey can trigger envy and regret as we recall lost opportunities or remember our own lost youth. While facing losses is a natural part of getting older, having them hurt the next generation will not alleviate them, and will only serve to create distance and hurt between the two of you.

Do not tease them about their boyfriends or girlfriends. If you do, it will close down conversation with them. Do not criticise them or get angry with them in front of their friends or other people. This is humiliating for them. Take them aside and talk to them in private. Teenagers feel more secure when they know they can rely on you to be in charge but you need to do so in a calm, gentle way.

10

Teenagers and Rules

How to Set Rules that Work for Everyone

What happens if all the positive communication strategies described in the previous chapter don't work? What do you do if you hit a brick wall and there's no willingness on your teenager's part to compromise? Sometimes, even with the best of intentions on your part, it is just not possible to find a solution where everyone's needs can be met. For whatever reason, negotiation just isn't working.

Your attempts to control your teenager's behaviour are obviously made with the best of intentions. You are trying to get them to change their behaviour, so that they avoid the painful consequences of their actions. You nag them to get them to sleep, eat, exercise, get organised, be tidy, study – all in an effort to help them avoid the pain of suffering the consequences of their actions. You may have realised at this point that trying to control what they do, so that they avoid the negative consequences, is not working. Instead, it merely results in creating conflict between you, or prevents them learning to take responsibility for themselves. It is good to remind yourself (even though you might not wish to admit it) that you cannot actually control the actions of others, and especially the actions of your children or teenagers. All you can do is change how you respond to what they do.

So, what can you do differently? Try to determine if the behaviour you would like them to change is genuinely an oversight or a mistake on their part. Are they distracted or forgetful, or is their attention elsewhere? Do they need help getting organised? (This may be why they seem to be ignoring your request to change.)

Natural Consequences

If it is clear that your teenager is genuinely trying to change, remember that one of the best ways to help them change is to allow them to experience the natural consequences of their actions, for example, going out in chilly weather without a jacket, forgetting to do homework, or failing to remember to bring a lunchbox to school. Normally, by experiencing these natural consequences they learn to become more organised and competent. When you were a teenager if you had not had the opportunity to experience the consequences of your own actions, you may not have learned all you have, and not have the wisdom you have today.

As explained in Chapter 7, teenagers (and indeed all humans) are motivated to move towards pleasure and away from pain. When we experience pleasure from an activity, we create a positive pattern-match with it, so that in the future we have an expectation of pleasure if we repeat that particular behaviour. The same mechanism is at play with pain. If we experience pain as a result of an action or a behaviour, we create a negative pattern-match, and we anticipate pain each time we repeat that action or behaviour. In this way, consequences motivate us to repeat behaviours that are pleasurable and avoid behaviours that are painful. They are a natural phenomenon: we reap what we sow.

ASK YOURSELF

Do you help your teenager too much by taking responsibility for their timekeeping, their lunch or their sports gear? Do you try to avoid them getting into trouble with their school or their sports coach for forgetting their belongings? Or are you willing to let your teenager learn from the consequences of their actions? It is only natural that you would want to avoid seeing your teenager experience pain, get into trouble and be miserable, but are you trying to protect them too much? Are you taking too much responsibility for them and not allowing them to learn for themselves?

If your teenager's mistake is genuine, you could investigate ways to help them pay more attention and be more focused. You could set up systems and strategies to help them get organised, such as using the 'reminders' function on their phone or a time-management application (there are a number of apps and software packages available). While such tools are interesting and useful, remind yourself that, ultimately, it is your teenager's responsibility to learn to manage their life.

Protecting your teenager too much stops them learning and growing, and if you take responsibility they will let you. They will assume that you will make sure that everything is okay, and then, when it is not, they will blame you. If you take responsibility for getting them to school on time, they don't have to keep an eye on the clock and ensure that they are not arriving late. Instead, you end up taking all that stress on your own shoulders. You need to let them make their own choices (within reason), even if you don't agree with them. Allow them to learn from their own mistakes. If their decision turns out to have unfortunate consequences, they will learn from it; just resist the urge to let them know you were right in the first place.

Helping teenagers to make changes by allowing them to fail can be tough. It means that you have to resist taking responsibility for them – something you probably have done all their lives – so that they learn to take responsibility for themselves. But you need to do this in stages, because if they haven't taken responsibility for themselves up until now, you will need to teach them gradually. For example, you could start with getting to school on time. Let them know that you will call them once or twice in the morning to get up, but that's it. If they don't get up in time, then *you* have to accept that they will be late for school. Once they have learned that, you could move on to the next thing, such as their lunchbox. Again let them know that you won't be running after them with their lunchbox should they forget to bring it with them – hunger will serve as a great motivator to help them remember to bring their lunchbox with them in future. While refusing to rescue them when they fail may seem harsh, what you are actually doing is very useful: you are teaching them to take responsibility for themselves by experiencing the consequences of their mistakes.

They will also test you out to see if you really stick to the consequences. This is the time to stay firm and hold your nerve. Trust that they will learn for themselves sooner or later – hopefully sooner. Carrying through on a consequence is actually doing them a favour. Even though they don't realise it, you are teaching them in a kind way. The big bad world beyond your front door may not be so kind.

For example, Sarah (16) doesn't tell you when she won't be home for dinner. You cook some food, expecting her to be there. Hours later, she saunters in without offering an apology. Ideally, from your side, the conversation could go like this:

'Sarah, I get frustrated and annoyed when you don't let me know that you will be late for dinner. It is giving the younger ones the message that it is okay to behave in that way. I need you to let me know at least one hour before dinner that you won't be here. Otherwise, I will give your dinner to the dog. If it continues to happen, I will stop including you when I am cooking the evening meal, and you will have to cook your own dinner.'

Remember, the rule is: state how you feel about the behaviour, ask for a specific change, spell out the consequences and then stick to them.

Setting the Rules

If you have tried many times to be reasonable and request a change in your teenager's behaviour and they seem to ignore you or they even just flatly refuse – or if they want to do something that is clearly dangerous – it is time to set rules and spell out the consequences of breaking those rules.

We have developed rules in society to ensure that everyone gets their needs met, and we all need rules to help us behave responsibly. Teenagers are at a stage in their lives when they naturally rebel against rules and, obviously, this can cause conflict. Examine the rules within your home. Are they clear and explicit or are they assumed? Rules and expectations need to be clear and specific, so that no one can hide behind the confusion of an assumption, or claim ignorance of an implied rule. Spell out the detail of the rules. For example: 'You must be home by 9 p.m. on school nights, and by 10 p.m. on weekends.' This works better than 'Be home at a reasonable hour.'

Involve Your Teenagers in Setting the Rules

Involve your teenager (or teenagers) in both setting the rules and agreeing the consequences of breaking those rules. Indeed, they may want to have their own input and add in rules about their privacy, their siblings 'borrowing' their belongings, their bedtimes, what they eat, etc.

Consequences for Breaking the Rules

Make the consequence fit the rule. If a consequence is seen as out of proportion to the broken rule, your teenager will feel aggrieved and they will not learn from it. Also, the consequence should not be too far into the future. If it is, you will merely be providing your teenager with sufficient time to try to manipulate you into backing down. Make it more immediate. Stopping them going to a party in a month's time is probably too far into the future, whereas stopping them going to the cinema tomorrow might work better.

You *must* follow through on the consequences for breaking the agreed rules. If you do not, the rules will not be taken seriously.

Ask yourself, who does their behaviour impact? If, for example, you want them to tidy their bedroom, remember that a messy, untidy room doesn't necessarily bother them, it only bothers you, so you need a consequence that impinges on them. One solution might be to close the door so that you don't see the mess, and leave it to them to experience the resulting chaos. Tell them that from now on you won't enter the room to tidy it or pick up their clothes for washing. Doing their own washing will soon become tedious, and they are therefore more likely to choose to comply with tidying their room for the sake of having an easier life. But, if they don't tidy their room, console yourself with the knowledge that you will have less laundry to do.

However, there is nothing more frustrating than to agree rules with your teenager and then to have them ignored by another adult who is involved in looking after them. So, once you have set down the rules and the consequences, it is important that all the adults directly involved in the teenager's upbringing (including your spouse/partner, relatives, grandparents or other adults) are aware of the rules you have devised and agree to them. Do not be surprised if some of the other adults involved take issue with you about what they deem appropriate as not everyone will share your ideas. Once the rules have been agreed and everyone has been made aware of them, responsibility for ensuring that the rules are kept rests with you as the parent(s). If you are not consistent with this, you won't be taken seriously.

Managing Rule-Breaking

When your teenager breaks a rule, either through a mistake or through sheer defiance, how you handle this can make a large difference to the outcome. If the only way you handle dealing with their mistakes is to mete out punishment, then you will only succeed in engendering shame, fear or anger in your teenager. Worse, you may indirectly teach them to cheat, lie and be sneaky, so as to avoid shame. They may learn to deny responsibility in order to avoid the shame of being wrong; they will feel hard done by and blame others. They will learn nothing useful, and fear will become the only motivation for compliance.

Teaching them how to take responsibility for their behaviour is much more difficult. Facing the consequences of their actions is much more painful than blaming someone else. For any of us – adults and teenagers alike – it is painful to reflect on our behaviour and be aware of the pain we may have caused others. It is much easier to lash out and blame someone else, which is why so many people do it. Taking responsibility makes us feel bad. We want our past mistakes to disappear and to forget that they ever happened. On the other hand, if we treat these mistakes as a *learning opportunity*, we will help our teenager mature. They will be more likely to stay calm and reflect on what they could have done differently and learn from their mistake.

> **ASK YOURSELF**
>
> Can you admit your own mistakes? Doing this can make it much easier for your teenager to admit theirs. It becomes no big deal, because all humans make mistakes.

If they admit to having made a mistake, give them lots of praise. Let them know that it takes a very mature person to own up to their failings. Moreover, it shows great strength of character. Teach your teenagers to take pride in doing the right thing. If, however, they refuse to admit to doing something wrong when you know they have done it, don't push it too much, either. Rather, just gently let them know you know they did it and they can tell you the truth when they are ready. If they subsequently tell you the truth, don't reproach them; tell them you are proud of them for owning up, as it is a really tough thing to do.

Once they have owned up, they will also need to 'clean up their mistake'. They will need to repair the damage and make amends for the hurt they caused. Making amends actually helps them to feel better and allows them to learn for the future. After they have cleaned up their mistake, let the matter go, and resist any temptation to remind them of the incident. They have made amends and it is time to move on. Reminding them or teasing them further will be of no benefit.

TWO OR MORE TEENAGERS?

If your household comprises more than one teenager, you will have the added stress of sibling rivalry. Siblings often have very contradictory feelings towards each other; it is totally normal. They can be really close, but they can also drive each other mad. They can be very caring and insanely envious and resentful of each other at the same time, and they are also likely to compete for your attention.

Some teenagers can get a kick out of teasing other siblings; it creates excitement and drama and can be an unhealthy way to meet their need for status and attention. In fact, it is sometimes the way family members relate to each other. But it can be really hurtful, and the unfortunate target who is being teased can then be the one to get into trouble for acting out emotionally.

All children, no matter what their age, have differing needs. Some need more support emotionally, others need practical help, independence or more privacy. Seeing your teenagers through the lens of their needs allows you to respond to each appropriately without having to worry about being fair to them all. Spend time alone with each of your teenagers. They will respond well to having exclusive time with you. Be interested in what interests them: this will help them feel secure and it will meet their need for attention. Hopefully, they will then be less likely to be envious of the attention you give to the other children in the family.

If they are upset or angry with one of their siblings, it is a good idea to let them express what they feel. Try to listen without judging or excusing the other child's behaviour. This will help them feel that you have heard their side of things, and that you understand how they feel. It can help them to let it go and they will therefore be less likely to retaliate. If you notice that one teenager is being particularly nasty to another, look for possible reasons behind it. Don't ignore it. Bring it out in the open and deal with it. Siblings can be quite hurtful to one another if they don't manage to keep their envy and anger in check (see Chapter 17).

When things are fraught in a family and you are genuinely doing your best, it may feel impossible to try to put yourself in your teenager's shoes and not react emotionally. Sometimes you feel *they* need to see things from *your* point of view for a change. Look for ways you can change what you do to improve matters rather than trying to force them to change. It is always easier to change your own approach than that of others.

If you are finding it difficult to stick to consequences, you may realise that all parents want to be liked by their teenagers but this can get in the way of parenting them. Do what you can to get your own needs for friendship and attention met through other adults in your life. If you do not manage to have these needs met, it can leave you vulnerable to becoming dependent on your teenagers for approval. This can jeopardise your decision-making and leave you susceptible to being manipulated by them. Your job is to parent them, not to be their friend. Remember, you set rules in order to protect your teenagers and avoid potentially disastrous or even fatal consequences. They may not be pleased with you today, but they will thank you in the long run.

11

Teenagers and Health

Physical Needs

We are all aware that we have physical needs of healthy air, water, food, sleep, shelter, exercise, etc., and that without these we will be physically unwell. By ensuring our physical needs are met, we can develop resilience and increase our immunity. Two of these needs that are frequent areas of conflict, food and exercise, are discussed further below. Sleep is discussed separately in Chapter 12 as this is an issue that often does not get the attention it deserves.

Food and Healthy Eating

Parents are often concerned about their teenager's diet – whether they are eating well, eating enough or eating too much. The teenage years are a time when the many changes that are occurring in an adolescent's body and brain can cause changes in eating habits and behaviours. As highlighted in earlier chapters, these years also coincide with a period when the adolescent is becoming their own person, choosing what clothes they wear and who they hang out with, and their interests and hobbies become increasingly important to them. Remember, this is also a period in their lives when they lose interest in things they used to like. So, they may change what they want to do in the way of hobbies, interests, sports, clothes, food choices, body piercings, hairstyles and so on. Respect their choices (provided they are safe).

Needing Independence

Everyone has an emotional need for control and autonomy, and this becomes more pronounced during the teenage years. Teenagers are forging their own identities and becoming themselves; they need to feel in control of their own lives. This is often expressed through food choices and eating patterns, so what and when teenagers eat can also become an important way for them to assert their independence and be autonomous.

It is normal and natural for teenagers to want to break away from their family, do things differently, and not be told what to do. They believe they 'know everything', and so they will rebel against much of what you say or do. This can result in making food a battleground – particularly if you want to influence what they eat. While they may be open to receiving information, taking advice from a parent is another thing altogether.

Managing or improving a teenager's diet can be tricky. It can be very difficult for adults to convince teenagers of the benefits of healthy eating while those teenagers are being simultaneously bombarded by powerful messages from food companies, advertisers and the media (about the 'desirability' of slimness or bodybuilding). When the effects of the influences of their peers are added into this mix, it is not easy for teenagers to resist these pressures and make healthy food choices.

As teenagers become aware of the many variations of diets that are out there, they begin to make choices about what they want to eat. One option might be to become a vegetarian. They may make this choice for a variety of reasons; for some it's from a deep concern about the welfare of animals, for others it's a fad that is fashionable among celebrities or their peers. Teenagers do need to be able to choose for themselves, but they also need information on how to maintain a nutritious diet, and the best source of this information is you, the parent.

If you are aware of the factors that can contribute to changes in your teenagers' eating behaviour, it can help you to determine whether the changes you are observing are something to be concerned about or not.

- *Biological changes:* Just like when a child is young and is experiencing a growth spurt – which results in them eating more – a similar phenomenon occurs during the teenage years. Adolescents may start eating food in amounts that will sometimes astound you. An hour after consuming a healthy meal, they will be back in the kitchen making sandwiches or cheese on toast, telling you they are 'starving'. This pattern may continue until they have finished a particular growth spurt, at which point they will begin to eat less. Such fluctuations in teenagers' eating habits are normal.

- *Self-consciousness, appearance and attention:* Teenagers can become painfully self-conscious, completely focused on how they appear to others, and whether or not they are regarded as attractive. This self-consciousness is driven by hormones: vasopressin and testosterone (for boys), and oestrogen and progesterone (for girls) (see Chapter 7).

Eating Away from Home More Often

For both adults and children, having friends and being part of a group meets an emotional need. A normal expression of meeting this need is eating out with friends. Indeed, one of mankind's most ancient customs is to share a meal with others. For teenagers, meeting this need could mean that they prefer to eat with their friends and may not want to eat with the family in the evening. Having a good social network is hugely important to a teenager's emotional health, and not eating at home once or twice a week will not cause any problems other than a drain on their or your finances. In fact, it could serve to increase their independence. It does mean that parents have less control over what their teenagers are eating when they are out, but this is all part of the 'letting go' process that every parent must learn to cope with.

As their need for friendship and belonging to a group is so important, it can mean that they regard being with their friends as more important than eating and may end up skipping meals to spend time with friends – which can be infuriating if you have prepared a meal for them. Remember teenagers are so caught up in their own lives they completely forget that certain decisions they make may have a major impact on other people. While bearing this in mind and being understanding of their needs, it is also important to have clear rules that encourage and teach respect and consideration for others – whether that be in relation to food and mealtimes, or in relation to other issues (see Chapter 10).

If your teenager is skipping meals in order to lose weight, that is another matter entirely. Skipping meals actually hinders weight loss. It also upsets the teenager's metabolism and sends the body into starvation mode. Breakfast is the meal most commonly skipped and that is definitely not a good idea. Many research studies have shown that breakfast helps to 'kick-start' the metabolism, thus getting the day off to a good beginning. The fuel that breakfast provides is important for enabling concentration at school during the morning. Indeed, some schools are so aware of this that they have established 'breakfast clubs' to ensure that all students have access to a healthy breakfast.

What You Can Do

The place to begin is with yourself and your own behaviour. It is important to set a good example. Your teenagers have been looking to you for guidance for many years. The most powerful messages they have received from you may not have been the direct ones; they may have been the indirect ones. So, your own relationship with your body and food is the best place to start if you want to send healthy eating messages to your teenager. If you want your teenager to eat more fruit and vegetables you need to ensure you eat enough of these foods yourself. If you don't follow your own advice, why should your teenager? If you are concerned about your own weight and decide to go on a diet, frame your reasons for doing so in terms of health rather than appearance. Rather than complaining that you look fat and you need to cut out sweet things, talk about how eating healthier food gives you more energy and makes you feel better and less run down.

Ensure that you stock a range of healthy foods in your kitchen, including a wide choice of food from all food groups – grains, vegetables, fruit, dairy, meat and fish. Have some food in store that can be used as snacks, preferably drawn from the above food groups. Avoid buying junk food, but, periodically, have some foods that teenagers enjoy in stock. Teenagers look for energy boosts. They will invariably look for quick and easy food. When they open the fridge and say, 'There's nothing to eat', try not to react. Remember what they are actually saying is, 'There is nothing really fast and sugary that I want to eat in the fridge', so try to ensure that you stock quick, easy foods that they can snack on such as fruit and nuts.

What Helps?

Try to avoid giving too much attention to your teenager's appearance, and focus instead on their other qualities. Remember they themselves can be overly focused on how they appear. Saying things like 'That was very thoughtful of you', 'You studied really well for that exam' or 'You showed great determination in your sports practice' will remind them of all their other attributes and help them balance their perception of themselves.

When it comes to changes in a teenager's body and appearance, help them to see these as a natural and normal part of maturing, and remind them that each person matures at a different rate. Avoid teasing them, or allowing family members to tease them about any changes they are experiencing, and remember just how self-conscious they are about their appearance. Teasing and making fun of a teenager can be very hurtful and upsetting, and could result in them developing a distorted view of their body.

When it comes to food, your teenager may have very different views to you, and getting into a battle about what they eat is counterproductive and will only damage your relationship with them. If, however, you are seriously concerned about them going on a dangerous or life-threatening diet, it is time to seek help (for more on this topic, see Chapter 20).

Get Them to Cook

Include your teenagers in the kitchen – both cooking and clearing up. Teach them to cook. It is a great way to connect with them, and it provides an opportunity for you to give them encouragement and praise. It's also a good way for them to learn about different food combinations, what flavours work well together and how to create a filling and nutritious meal out of a few odd ingredients. Involve them in all aspects of food preparation – from planning and shopping to preparing and cooking. Let them experiment with different types of cooking. Remember, you are teaching them a skill for life, so that they will be able to fend for themselves when they leave home and will not have to rely on fast food and takeaways.

Don't just focus on the girls. Involve your boys (both teenagers and younger children) in cooking as well; use the fact that your son's status will be increased among his peers and with potential girlfriends if he can cook well. It will also boost his self-confidence.

Support and Guidance

Do support your teenager as they make choices in their own food preferences. But, if you are concerned about certain behaviours, such as dieting or bingeing, it is important to seek professional help. Start with your GP, who may put you in touch with a professional who is expert in the area of nutritional or psychological advice.

Most teenagers manage to navigate their way through the myriad of food choices available, and they succeed in developing a balanced view of food. Try not to be too focused on their choices. Instead, try to focus on helping them to feel good about themselves through having challenging and stretching goals to aim for. This will focus them on other areas of their lives and enable them to understand that while appearance is important, there are more satisfying ways to achieve increased self-esteem. This in turn will make it less likely that they will indulge in harmful diets.

EXERCISE

Exercise delivers immense benefits (both physically and mentally) for people of all ages, and is particularly beneficial for teenagers. Sometimes when teenagers understand exactly how exercise benefits us, it serves as an incentive to encourage them to 'get physical', which helps them to cope better with all the hormonal changes and other life changes they are experiencing. Exercise tones your body, and makes you look and feel better, as well as delivering a long list of other amazing benefits. It can even boost brain function. This can be a great incentive for teenagers, as it offers an additional way for them to boost their grades. Let's look at the many benefits of exercise one by one:

- *Stress buster and anxiety alleviator:* Exercise is the great stress buster. When we exercise, we are doing what nature intended: we are burning up the energy that was produced by the stress response, and it also helps boost our ability to deal with stress in the future.

- *Mood changer:* Exercise lifts our mood and increases our sense of well-being. Whenever we exercise we cause the release of endorphins, the so-called happy chemicals. These create feelings of well-being and happiness, which is why we feel so good after going for a long walk or a run. Numerous research studies have shown that exercise on its own can alleviate the symptoms of mild depression, and this is the reason why many GPs now recommend that patients who are suffering from depression or anxiety go for a 30-minute walk every day.
- *Increased mental performance:* Exercise increases neurogenesis (the production of new brain cells), and it can improve overall mental performance. It increases the levels of the brain protein BDNF (brain-derived neurotrophic factor), which is believed to help support the survival of existing neurons and also encourages the growth of new neurons and synapses.
- *Improved memory:* When we exercise, the production of cells in the hippocampus is increased. This is the area of the brain that is responsible for memory and learning. Research has shown that there is a link between physical fitness and brain development.
- *Better sleep:* Moderate exercise can really help us sleep better; it can be as effective as taking a sleeping pill. One important point: exercise needs to be taken about five hours before bedtime. The reason is that when we exercise, our body temperature increases, and body-temperature decrease is a signal that it is time to sleep.
- *Helps overcome addiction:* The neurochemical dopamine is released in the brain in response to any pleasurable activity. This is part of the brain's reward system. Exercise is a pleasurable activity, and it can be used to replace the 'high' from drugs or alcohol.
- *Controlling weight gain and maintaining weight loss:* Exercise helps to control weight gain and to maintain weight loss.
- *Stronger bones:* Regular moderate exercise – especially exercise that is weight-bearing such as walking or jogging – increases your bone density, strengthening your bones and protecting you from osteoporosis in later life.
- *Better skin:* Physical activity boosts circulation. Increased circulation delivers nutrients to the skin and helps eliminate toxins

(poisons). It also boosts the delivery of oxygen to the skin, which in turn increases collagen and is responsible for the elasticity and strength of the skin.

- *Strengthened immune system:* Exercise strengthens your immune system, thus helping you deal with colds, flus and other viruses more effectively.
- *Energy booster:* Regular exercise delivers oxygen and nutrients to your body more efficiently, with the result that you have *more* energy, not less.
- *Exercise can be fun and it can help ensure your emotional needs are met:* If you find the right exercise for you, it can be an enjoyable way to spend time. It can help you connect with family or friends in a social setting. It may even serve to help you make new friends and give you a sense of community.
- *Increased productivity:* Research shows that students who take a break and go for a short walk or a run get more done and are more productive than those who stay glued to their books. Plus, given that exercise increases memory function and boosts brainpower, incorporating it into a study routine makes a lot of sense.
- *Creativity booster:* Moving your body can boost your creativity through refreshing both your body and your brain. People often come up with better ideas after they have been out for a walk or a run.
- *Inspiring others:* When you exercise, you indirectly inspire others to follow your lead, as, deep down, we all know that exercise is good for us.

Given all the benefits associated with exercise, it makes sense for both you and your teenager to incorporate it into your daily life. As a general goal, aim to engage in at least 30 minutes of physical activity every day and, if you cannot do an actual workout, get more active throughout the day in simple ways, e.g. walk or cycle to school, or get off the bus two stops early and walk the rest of the way.

What Kind of Exercise?

First and foremost, the exercise anyone chooses must be enjoyable, and it must meet their needs. One of the main reasons why people give up a particular exercise is because it no longer meets a need and ceases to be enjoyable. When choosing an exercise, try to match it with your or your teenager's personality. Think about what suits. So if your teenager is more of an introvert, exercising on their own might work better as it gives them time to themselves and meets their need for privacy – for example, swimming or running. On the other hand, a teenager who is more extroverted may be more suited to team sports because it gives them an opportunity to spend time with other people, and meets their need to belong to a group – for example, soccer, hurling or other sports that are group-orientated, such as tennis or martial arts.

The goal for all of us is a long-term internalisation of the pleasure and benefits of exercise. Students often drop exercise when they come to their exam years, feeling that they don't have time and that they need to study. Unfortunately, sticking with or quitting an exercise routine at this point may determine whether they will remain active through to adulthood. We see the same phenomenon in adults, who despite knowing that exercise is good for them also give up their exercise routine due to work commitments and family responsibilities – and they subsequently see their stress levels increase.

Paradoxically, one of the ways to beat the effects of stress – and the consequent poor decisions made as a result of being stressed – is to remove the choice element in the exercise equation. Most of us tend not to wonder whether we have time for sleeping or eating – it's a given. In contrast, many of us wonder whether we can spare the time to take exercise – it's a choice. The fact is, if exercise were part and parcel of your daily routine, as opposed to something you choose to do or not do, you would be more likely to continue. So get out and be active – and make sure your teenagers are active. Physical health has a huge impact on mental health, and when viewed in that light, the decision to take regular exercise is no longer a choice. It's a *must*.

The best way to motivate your teens is to set a good example. As highlighted in earlier pages, you may not realise it, but they are hugely influenced by what they see. They pay huge attention to what you *do*, not to what you *say*. If you yourself are a model of healthy eating and exercise, there is a much better chance that they will follow your lead. There are no guarantees, of course, but you are increasing the likelihood that they will favour more healthy choices. Partake in regular physical activity, such as walking or cycling, instead of using the car for short trips, and encourage them to do likewise.

What if My Teenager Doesn't Like Sports?

Exercise doesn't need to be in the form of a sport as such, as not all teenagers are interested in sports. Walking or cycling to or from school constitutes exercise: the most important thing is to get your body moving. It is a physical need. Perhaps, for your teenager, other extra-curricular activities that involve movement would be more appropriate. Music, drama or dance, for instance, all deliver benefits that can help a young person to move and transition through the teenage years.

12

TEENAGERS AND SLEEP

We are all aware that sleep is important, and that lack of sleep can be detrimental to both our physical and psychological well-being. When it comes to teenagers, the amount of time they spend sleeping (either too much or too little) is often a source of concern. Research into the function of sleep is ongoing, and scientists are constantly learning more about the regulatory role of sleep and dreaming in our lives. While there are still many unanswered questions, we now have a much greater understanding of what happens during sleep, and why is it so vital.

When we sleep, we are not just resting; it is an active process and our brain is busy at work. There are two main types of sleep: non-rapid eye movement (NREM) sleep (also known as quiet sleep or slow wave sleep), and rapid eye movement (REM) sleep (also known as active sleep or paradoxical sleep). Sleep goes through stages, based on changes in the brain's electrical activity, and these stages are repeated in cycles throughout the night.

Sleep commences with a relatively light stage of NREM – where we drift from normal wakefulness into sleep, and brain activity slows as we relax and drift off. As we fall into deeper sleep, our muscles relax, our body temperature drops, our heart rate slows and our brains produce slow (delta) waves as we move into deep sleep. These deep-sleep stages are extremely important, as it is during these stages that the body repairs and regenerates tissue, builds bone and muscle, and strengthens the immune system. During these periods, the brain cells are also recharged with sugars, thus refreshing the brain for the challenges of the upcoming day. We then move into REM sleep, so called due to presence of the characteristic eye movement that takes place at this point. REM sleep is sometimes referred to as 'paradoxical sleep' because, during this phase, while the brain becomes more active, the muscles of the body become more relaxed. It is during this stage that dreaming occurs, which creates increased brain activity – similar to the level of activity that takes place during wakefulness.

Throughout the night, a person with a healthy sleep pattern repeats the various stages of sleep in a particular sequence. For example, at the start of the night, they will experience a longer period of NREM sleep for approximately 90 minutes, followed by about 10 minutes of REM sleep. With each subsequent sleep cycle, the amount of REM sleep increases. The final cycle will have up to 60 minutes' REM sleep, and occurs just prior to waking.

This pattern presents differently in people who are depressed; such individuals experience more REM sleep, starting earlier in the night, and less NREM sleep throughout the night. The increased brain activity of the REM stage early in the night, along with the reduction in the restorative NREM stages, means that they wake feeling tired, with the sense that they have not slept well, even though they may have actually slept for eight to ten hours. This accounts for the lack of motivation and energy in those who are depressed.

The important issue in relation to sleep is not only to get the correct *amount* of sleep, but also the correct balance in terms of *sleep mix*. Teenagers often don't get enough sleep or the right *mix* of sleep, i.e. they don't achieve the right balance between NREM and REM sleep. The main function of NREM sleep is repair and refreshment (where the body and brain are restored and provided with the requisite energy for a new day). The role of REM sleep is quite different: it is during this stage of sleep that we do most of our dreaming. Dreaming sleep burns a lot of energy, and during this phase our brains are almost as active as they are when we are awake. Research shows that dreaming is the brain's way of processing the emotionally charged events of the day; in particular those events where we failed to express our emotions. It is as if these unexpressed emotional events have been waiting to be completed and when we dream we have the opportunity to express these emotions and 'complete the event'. In short, dreaming has the effect of flushing out the debris of the day's concerns and equipping us to face the next day's events.

Take, as an example, the internal emotional turmoil experienced by any teenager who has a crush on someone who is completely oblivious to their attention. The poor teenager may have spent hours that day anxiously contemplating their appearance, agonising about what they have said or done, and how this was interpreted by the object of their affection. All of this anxiety and turmoil has to be processed later that night while dreaming: the more rumination the teenager does, the more dreaming will be required in order to flush out all that anxiety and turmoil.

Taking into account the huge emotional upheavals of the teenage years, coupled with the stress of a changing body and the young person's search for their own identity, we can perhaps begin to appreciate the level of youngsters' emotionally arousing concerns. Unless these emotionally charged concerns are expressed during the day (which they often are), the teenager will need to 'complete' these concerns at night, in their dreams. Indeed, the more stress and frustration that is experienced by any of us at any age that is not expressed during the day, the more dreaming we will need to do at night.

From a health point of view, the more REM sleep we have on a given night, the less NREM sleep we will have, which in turn results in us feeling tired and unmotivated the following day. Rumination over the worries of the day – be they socially related worries, or worries about academic or sporting performance – all cause an increase in REM sleep. We can manage our sleep better when we understand this connection between rumination and REM sleep. If you feel exhausted after a night's sleep, the probability is that you have been doing a lot of REM sleep. Reducing rumination will result in reducing REM sleep and will lead to a more refreshing sleep. This further underlines the importance of introducing activities into your life that absorb your attention and thus prevent rumination.

Falling Asleep and Body Clocks

Your brain uses external cues to set an internal clock (known as the circadian clock) that controls your sleep patterns and other body functions. Such patterns and functions all follow an approximately 24-hour cycle, known as a circadian rhythm, which is regulated by external cues such as light, temperature, eating patterns, social interactions and other habits. These cues tell your brain where you are in your daily sleep/waking cycle.

Your internal clock is a little group of cells located in the hypothalamus in your brain. These signals trigger the release of melatonin, a hormone that helps regulate the sleep cycle. The cells in the hypothalamus receive signals from the eyes. Darkness causes the hypothalamus to produce melatonin, whereas bright light triggers the cessation of the production of melatonin. That is why exposure to early-morning light helps you to wake up, and why it is harder to wake in winter, when the mornings are darker. The night-time use of smartphones and other electronic devices (which emit strong light close to the eyes) can dampen melatonin production and, consequently, can have an adverse effect on falling asleep. This is particularly important for teenagers who are constantly using screens, often right up to bedtime, and while in bed.

CASE STUDY: ROSE AND HER TEMPER

Rose was twelve and attending a local school when her behaviour began to cause huge problems for her classmates and teacher. She couldn't seem to control her anger. She would blow up at any contentious interaction. She would hit other children, kick the teacher, throw her books or pencils at others, and was even known to throw her chair around the room.

Her family background was far from ideal. She was living with her aunt, as her mother had formed a new relationship and was now living in another part of the country. Rose had no contact with her father. Initially, I had assumed that being separated from her mother was the cause of her anger, but in reality this didn't seem to bother her, as she was very close to her aunt and her grandmother. Following one or two sessions, she had made some progress, but she was still finding it hard to manage her anger. Poor Rose was very upset about this: she really did want to behave better. A chance remark caused me to ask her about her sleep patterns. Her aunt had taken over her parenting when Rose was about nine years old, and Rose went to live with her in her apartment. Recently, her aunt had begun to work at a local restaurant in the evenings, and Rose would go to her grandmother's house until her aunt finished work. Rose saw no point in going to sleep until her aunt came home from work, as she would only have to wake up and go home when she got in. This meant that Rose wasn't getting to sleep until about midnight on the nights when her aunt was working. The simple truth was that Rose wasn't getting enough sleep. As Rose's aunt had only recently taken over her parenting, she was completely unaware of how much sleep a twelve-year-old needed, and was visibly upset when she realised that she had inadvertently been neglectful in this way. I designed an experiment to see if a change in Rose's sleeping arrangements would make a difference. It resulted in a marked change in her behaviour at school: she looked better, performed better, and found that she could be calm even when her classmates bothered her or when the teacher pointed out an error in her schoolwork. Rose was delighted and proud of herself: she had learned a valuable lesson about the importance of one of our crucial physical needs – sleep!

So, What Is Different about the Sleep Patterns of a Teenager?

Brain activity during sleeping hours changes as we move from childhood to adolescence. The intensity of brain activity during NREM sleep decreases by approximately 65 per cent during the teenage years. This decrease occurs at a time in the teenager's development when the synapses of the brain are also being formed, strengthened and pruned at a huge rate – a rate surpassing that of adulthood. As this is such a crucial developmental period for a teenager, the effect of disrupted or insufficient sleep is increased. It may be that the brain's pruning and strengthening changes are affected by sleep loss, thus resulting in forgetfulness or misjudgement.

To understand the science of sleep, it is important to understand the significance – and the importance – of the role played by melatonin. First, a few facts. Melatonin levels are lower in adolescents than they are in children or adults. More significantly, the time of night when melatonin levels reach their peak shifts to a later hour during the adolescent years. Both these factors make it more difficult for a teenager to fall asleep earlier at night. So, when you notice that your teenager has begun to stay up late and wake up later each morning, it is not because they are simply being defiant. When teenagers want to stay up late and get up late, they are doing so because they are being affected by changes in their melatonin levels. They seem to need about nine hours' sleep, and when they are allowed to sleep as long as they want this is the amount of time they average. Often, they don't get enough sleep – as they have too much homework to do, are engaged in socialising, are playing video games and so on – and, to them, sleep may just seem like a waste of time.

The problem is, however, that too little sleep – particularly on school nights – causes increased levels of the stress hormone cortisol. Sleep-deprived teenagers exhibit exaggerated stress responses, which interfere with their daily activities and can also affect school performance. And, of course, for both teenagers and adults alike, falling asleep can be difficult if they are feeling stressed or anxious.

Many sleep experts believe that one of the effects of the changes in melatonin levels and times of release during the teenage years is that adolescents go into a period of sleep debt during the week – a consequence of falling asleep late at night, followed by having to get up early for school the next morning. As a result, getting extra sleep at the weekend is good for them if they are not getting a full nine hours' sleep during the week. This 'catch-up' sleep works for some teenagers. But, for others, a change in sleeping times at the weekend may make it harder for them to readjust to the weekday sleep pattern, thus causing them further stress.

Many scientists now believe that a change in school start times (aimed at accommodating the negative effects of the change in teenagers' melatonin production) could go a long way towards reducing students' stress levels and increasing their performance levels. In fact, in schools where a later start time was introduced, student attendance improved and students were more likely to remain in full-time education beyond the age of sixteen; the school environment generally was calmer, and students displayed higher levels of alertness.

IMPORTANCE OF BEDTIME

Gone are the days when you could enforce a bedtime regime, as you did when your child was younger. Teenagers do not like being treated like children. By giving them the facts and explaining to them the reasons why sleep is so important you will be treating them like adults, which will help them take responsibility for their sleep.

Another factor to remember is that your teenager's frontal lobes are not yet fully formed and, as a consequence, they will not necessarily be good at planning their time. You may need to help them plan their evenings in such a way that they get a proper night's sleep and go to bed at a reasonable hour.

DIFFICULTIES IN FALLING ASLEEP

Teenagers who ruminate about their problems while they are in bed will find it more difficult to fall asleep easily, and will suffer anxiety and stress. Stress has a knock-on negative effect on sleep; therefore, try to ensure that whatever is causing your teenager undue stress is dealt with so that they don't end up with the additional stress of having to cope with a sleep problem.

Use the tips below to help your teenager find ways to calm their brains prior to bedtime. Difficulty in falling asleep, or staying asleep, may also be a sign of a more serious problem, such as substance abuse. Be aware of changes in your teenager's sleeping patterns.

TIPS FOR SLEEPING BETTER

Here are some ways to improve sleep. Some you may be already familiar with and some will work better for you/your teenager than others.

- Avoid caffeine in the afternoon and evening.
- Avoid drinking alcohol at night. While it can help in getting you off to sleep, it disrupts the later stages of sleep.
- Take exercise in the evening, but make sure that the exercise period does not take place too close to bedtime.
- Maintain a regular pre-bedtime routine, do the same things in the same order before bed. This provides cues to signal to your brain that it is time to sleep.
- Avoid being exposed to bright light, i.e. watching television, working on a bright computer screen or using a smartphone/tablet, up to one hour before bedtime.

- Avoid the urge to sleep excessively at the weekend, as it can result in making it that much harder to get to sleep on Sunday night and get up on Monday morning.
- Encourage and arrange activities on weekends that will get you and your teenagers up within an hour or two of your usual weekday rising time.
- Ensure that you have a comfortable mattress.
- Do not nap during the afternoon.
- If you are always tired in the morning and you go to bed late, work to change your routine by slowly bringing forward your bedtime.
- Make sure that you are neither too hot nor too cold in bed.
- Where possible, use the bedroom primarily for sleep, so that your brain makes the association between the bedroom and sleep. This may not be practical for teenagers, who often use their bedrooms for studying. If this is the case, encourage them to study at a desk and use their bed for sleeping only.

Try not to worry about whether you are sleeping or not. Worry and anxiety interfere with sleep, and sleep loss triggers more anxiety. Try to break that cycle. Remember that your brain interprets the act of worrying as its opportunity to problem-solve and by worrying you may be inadvertently rewarding your brain for staying awake.

OTHER SUGGESTIONS

- Try visualisation; some people use a relaxation recording or a visualisation to help them get to sleep.
- Pick a time to get up each morning, and stick to that time, no matter what.
- Do not go to bed until you are physically tired.
- If you are not asleep within 30 minutes, get up and do something that is extremely boring. This must be something (preferably quiet) that you really hate doing, something mundane, such as sorting out your sock drawer. This is the origin of the idea of counting sheep – a boring task helps send you to sleep. As soon as you are tired, abandon the task and go to bed.

- If you are still awake after another 30 minutes, get up and do another extremely boring task.

The part of your brain that controls sleep is primitive and stupid. Like a pet animal, it can be trained through reward and punishment. If it realises that instead of being rewarded for waking up, it ends up doing tasks it hates, it will quickly learn to let you sleep through the night. It may take time to do this retraining, but the benefits of a good night's sleep are definitely worth the effort.

13

TEENAGERS AND STUDY

MOTIVATION

In earlier chapters we discussed how the brain learns through pattern-matching, i.e. through referring back to what it already knows and then adding to that store when it is exposed to new knowledge or information. We also discovered that curiosity and learning is our natural state; we come into the world curious about it and eager to learn about how it works. Stretching, learning, achieving and feeling competent are all innate emotional needs. So, what happens when this innate desire is thwarted and upset, and we become demotivated to learn? Why is it that some of us love school and learning, and some hate it? What makes the difference? Why is it that some teenagers are motivated to learn and some are not? Motivation is what causes us to act, and we will feel motivated to do something when we believe that by doing so our needs will be met.

The difference lies in our perception (or pattern-match) of school, learning, mistakes, failure, etc., and also of ourselves. What we perceive is not the object or activity itself, but the meaning we have attached to it. So our motivation and thoughts about learning are directly related to this meaning. The youngster who is not interested in learning perceives that school or study will not meet their needs. They have learned to attribute a negative meaning to school and learning and perhaps even to themselves. Similarly, motivated youngsters have attributed a meaning to school, learning and themselves – but a positive one – and this meaning is what makes the difference.

Carol Dweck, Professor of Psychology at Stanford University in California, has done extensive research on the topic of motivation. She investigates what motivates children to learn, and why it is that bright children often get stuck in their schooling and seem reluctant to challenge themselves to do better. We know from earlier chapters that the brain is a highly dynamic, malleable organ, which changes in response to new experiences. It is also shaped and changed by repetition, and it grows in response to repeated use. This is known as *brain plasticity*. What Carol Dweck has discovered is that understanding this phenomenon can greatly influence our motivation to stretch ourselves, take risks and learn.

Fixed Minds

Up until recently, scientists believed the brain stopped developing when a child was aged ten or thereabouts, and that whatever abilities and talents the child displayed at that age were fixed for life. From this perspective, categorising children and adults into groups with different intelligence levels, talents and skills would have made perfect sense: some were good at mathematics, some were good at languages, some were good at sport or art, and so on. But neuroscientific and psychological research has now proved that this view of people is incorrect. This misconception is borne out by the many stories of people who failed early in their careers, only to become hugely successful in their chosen fields later in life. Albert Einstein, Richard Branson and J.K. Rowling are some examples.

The old belief of having a fixed ability – or, as Dweck phrases it, a 'fixed mindset' – can cause many undesirable effects, whether that belief is that you have great abilities or that you have few. It may seem counterintuitive that believing you have great abilities can cause problems, but, as we will see, it can cause a person anxiety and create an unwillingness to challenge and stretch themselves.

Having a fixed mindset means that you believe your abilities are fixed and set. As a result, a person will live up or down to that perception, and will also feel a need to prove that belief to be correct. It creates great pressure on children who have been told they are very bright or talented, and can result in them having a need to prove their super-abilities over and over again. Making a mistake or looking deficient or inadequate will make them feel very insecure, and this pressure can create anxiety to prove themselves in school, in college and in work. If a child has been told they are 'smart' they are less likely to put effort into solving a difficult maths problem, as they believe that if they are smart the answer will just come to them. This means they won't reach their potential. Conversely, children who have been told directly or indirectly that they are slow will also try to meet this expectation and so will feel demotivated to stretch and learn.

Growing Minds

However, when we see the brain as 'plastic', it opens up all sorts of possibilities, and it changes our view of both learning and motivation. Dweck calls this perspective a 'growth mindset' and it is based on the fact that your basic qualities and abilities are aspects that you develop and cultivate through your own efforts. It is true that people do differ in their talents, aptitudes, interests or temperaments, but what we now realise is that everyone can *grow and change* through application of effort and experience. It is impossible to foretell what a person could accomplish if they were to invest years of effort and passion in a particular interest.

Dweck realised through her research that the mindset a youngster adopts – a fixed mindset of having a fixed ability (whether it was that they were bright or slow), or a growth mindset (of always learning and growing) – determines how they respond to challenges in life. A young person with a fixed mindset is more reluctant to take risks, challenge themselves and try out new things, so they are at a disadvantage when it came to learning and growing. The problem lies in their perception of what it means to make mistakes or fail in some way. The youngsters with fixed mindsets see mistakes as either confirmation that they are slow or as a threat to their intelligence. ('I'm not smart/gifted/talented after all!' or 'I knew I was stupid!') So they avoid challenges and anything where they might risk making a mistake and looking bad. This means they are less likely to stretch themselves and meet the challenges that all learning requires.

On the other hand, a youngster with a growth mindset approaches learning from a different perspective. They regard learning as a motivation to get better at whatever they do. They are focused on the process of learning rather than the result or the exam mark achieved at the end. They are interested in their deficiencies and in how to overcome them rather than being afraid or ashamed of them. If they get a low mark or lose a game, of course they will be upset, but they will also look to see how they can improve, how they can use this to do things differently next time. They will ask themselves questions such as 'Do I need to work harder, or in a different way?' or 'Am I concentrating on the wrong areas?' They want to grow and progress. They develop a passion for, and a love of, learning. They recognise intuitively that they need to stretch themselves, and that nothing beats the amazing feeling they get from feeling competent and achieving their goals.

WHAT IS YOUR MINDSET?

It is useful to question your own mindset. Do you believe that your own intelligence or talent is fixed, and that you cannot change? Do you believe that you cannot change your basic intelligence? Do you have a 'fixed mindset'?

Alternatively, do you believe that you can change how intelligent or talented you are? Do you believe that you can always learn and grow? That you can adapt and change even your personality traits if you choose to? Do you have a 'growth mindset'?

Can you be both? You might recognise that you have a fixed mindset in one area (such as sports), but a growth mindset in another area (such as academic performance or creativity). Becoming aware of your own mindset(s) can really open up possibilities in your own life.

What Dweck realised was that the view you adopt for yourself – the mindset you have – hugely determines whether you accomplish what you want in life. The fixed mindset keeps you stuck, creates anxiety and can even lead to depression. It focuses on a very fixed idea of an individual's abilities and talents. When things become challenging, this type of person loses interest, gets stressed and becomes anxious that they might fail. If their abilities are fixed, there is no way out. 'Why waste your time studying?' they say. They try to repair their self-esteem in other ways – cheating, blaming others, making excuses.

A growth mindset recognises that we are always learning. People with this mindset don't just seek out challenge – they thrive on it, which in turn creates hope and focuses their minds on effort. They know that failure doesn't define them: they use it to learn and grow. They know that failure means they lack competence, and that this can be rectified through effort. They are not afraid of mistakes. They are willing to take risks, put in effort and work hard to achieve what they want. The passion for stretching yourself and sticking to it – especially when the process is not going so well – is a key characteristic of someone with a growth mindset.

In Praise of Effort

The key to growth and development is effort. If you perceive yourself as intelligent, you may think that you shouldn't need to put in effort, that effort is only required by those who are not so clever. Putting in effort proves that you are not as intelligent as you thought you were. A fixed mindset like this can be hugely demotivating. Parents may not be aware that, even with the best of intentions, telling their children they are smart or clever can backfire in this way.

Try to observe what you tell your children. For example, are you implying that their traits are permanent? Or are you saying they are developing and growing, and that you are interested in how they are developing and growing? How do you praise? Praising a child's intelligence or talent gives them a fixed-mind message. Instead, try to focus on the effort your children have put into a particular endeavour. Focus on the strategies they used, their choices of study methods or practice.

Watch how you deal with their setbacks. Teach them to reflect on what they could have done differently, rather than reassure them they are brilliant, or put the responsibility on a bad teacher or a bad sports coach. Help them to focus on getting better at what they do. Help them to develop a growth mindset, as this mindset will be the foundation that will help them deal with the challenges of life – whether those challenges manifest in school, college, work, relationships or health. Focus on effort, and teach both yourself and your children to have a growth mindset. Develop a belief in change and take the focus off how you and they are seen by others.

Changing to a more flexible approach can take time. It challenges you to do things you might have found threatening in the past. It asks you to embrace risk and exert effort – perhaps struggle, get criticised, have setbacks – and it will possibly make you feel insecure. But, remember, this is what enables you to grow.

Try to nurture in your children the concept that when something is hard to do or solve, it is fun. This changes the meaning of failure from something that is shameful to something that is a step on the way to success.

ASK YOURSELF

How do I see success? If success is about proving something, you are seeing success from a fixed viewpoint, something static, e.g. 'I am smart. I am successful.' This leaves you vulnerable to something unexpected happening to threaten that viewpoint and the confidence you feel can be fragile and insecure. Alternatively, look at it from a different angle: 'Is success about learning? Is it about growing and stretching?' If viewed this way, it is easier to change setbacks into opportunities. People with this perspective have confidence in their ability to knuckle down and put in effort so that no matter what happens in their lives, they can view misfortune as a challenge and they can rely on themselves to resolve difficulties.

Teach your children to enjoy challenges and to be curious about mistakes. Support them in putting in effort and in learning – no matter what the results. That way, they will not be slaves to praise, and they will acquire a lifelong ability to build true confidence and repair that confidence if they get knocks in life. Praise your children for their *efforts*. Say: 'You worked really hard for that exam, and your results show it' or 'That idea of using index cards setting out the points you needed to remember for the exam paper has really paid off.' All of this advice applies equally to teenagers and young children.

Remember, during the adolescent years, teenagers are experimenting and trying out different personalities to figure out who they are, who they will become. They are also hugely concerned about how they are regarded by others, and one way of asserting independence from parents and adults is to rebel against their expectations. If you expect your teenagers to achieve high results, and if you only focus on their results, they may protect themselves by downing tools and not trying at all.

SELF-PERCEPTION AND THE ART OF REFLECTION

In general, most people find it difficult to acquire an accurate view of their own talents, but Dweck's studies showed that those people with a fixed mindset are the most *inaccurate* in their self-perception. This makes sense: the more you fear feedback, the less of it you will want to hear and you will want to protect your own perception of yourself. But if you are more concerned about *learning* than about *looking good*, you will be much more interested in what others have to say about your abilities – even if what they have to say is negative.

Dweck is not saying that all children are born equal. Certainly, there are gifted children and there are children who are born with fewer resources and opportunities than others. But what she is saying is that it is becoming increasingly clear that, with the right attitude and mindset, *we are all capable of achieving more than we think*. The interesting thing is that many people who focus on growth get to the top almost as a by-product. They concentrate on getting better at what they do and on increasing their expertise. They do it because they love it and they want to achieve mastery, not because they want to get to the top, or gain high status.

GOING TO COLLEGE

The transition from school to college or university is a vulnerable time, particularly if a teenager has been at the top of their class all through school. When they arrive at college, they will be mixing with other high achievers, and so they may be disappointed that they are no longer at the top of their class. If you have teenagers in this situation, perhaps you can now see how a focus on learning and effort will give them the tools they need to enjoy the challenge of college, and not get disheartened by failing to excel from the time they arrive. Believe in the concept of the growth of your child's brain, and let them know that it can feel difficult when your brain is growing and making new connections; it is no different from the way muscles can hurt when you exercise them after a period of disuse.

When your teenagers are disappointed with something, resist the urge to reassure them. Instead, if they are resentful about an outcome, help them to reflect on how to use their disappointment and resentment to do better next time. For example, perhaps they could work harder, be more helpful, or increase their commitment and effort. Most of all, try to get them to view effort as *enjoyable* and learning as *rewarding*. Not only will you be giving them one of life's most precious gifts, you will also be giving them resilience against the lure of the easy fix and the dangers of addiction.

STUDY AND MEMORY

A lot of time and effort can be wasted if we don't understand how to learn and how to study effectively. Knowing which methods have been proven to be effective and which are less so might surprise you, because most students stick to the methods they have developed over years and don't stop to consider whether there are more effective ways of studying. Reading and rereading material – hoping that you will remember the content – is one of the most common mistakes. We forget approximately 70 per cent of what we read or hear, and even if we reread the material that percentage doesn't change by much. Students continue to use this method despite the fact that it delivers poor results and takes a great deal of time. It can be a powerful way of persuading themselves that they know the material when, in fact, it has been shown that students who use this method are overconfident in their knowledge. *Feeling confident* and *demonstrating competence* in a subject are two totally different things.

All learning requires some level of prior knowledge; indeed, it is a precondition for making sense of a new topic. When you hear something new, you need to refer this new information back to what you already know, so that you can connect it in some way to knowledge you already have. For example, you need a basic understanding of numbers and their meaning before you can learn addition and subtraction, and you need to understand addition before you can make sense of multiplication, and so on. Your brain converts new material into mental representations or patterns. These patterns need to connect up to what you have already learned, and those connections need to be strengthened. The process of forming these connections is called consolidation. When we learn something new, it is fragile – its meaning or significance is not yet fully established in the brain. As it is not yet stable it can be easily lost. When learning is being consolidated and the connections are being formed, the brain strengthens and stabilises these patterns in long-term memory.

When we learn something initially it starts out disorganised but this consolidation helps to organise and crystallise it. Retrieval, the next stage, also helps to shape it. Retrieval strengthens the learning and makes it more flexible, so that it can be connected up to other knowledge. This is sometimes called reconsolidating. When students are studying, this process of encoding, consolidation, retrieval and reconsolidation becomes important. The ability to retrieve knowledge easily is vital when your knowledge is being assessed, or when you are sitting exams.

How to Increase Memory

What is the most effective way to develop the ability to retrieve knowledge when needed? We know that rereading is not particularly effective. However, we also know that regular retrieval through methods such as self-testing or being quizzed by someone greatly improves our ability to retain and retrieve material. Retrieval strengthens learning. But students often don't like being tested or quizzed, and while this is totally understandable (because no one likes to be seen to fail) it has several advantages over reading and rereading. It helps the student realise what they know and what they don't know by giving them immediate feedback. Students who use testing and retesting perform better at exams and also find that they need to do less revision.

How does testing or quizzing affect learning? The immediate feedback of what they can and cannot remember allows the student to focus on what they do *not* know, instead of spending more time on what they *do* know, a common mistake. They actually learn and remember *more* than students who restudied the material without being tested. They have a more accurate idea of what they know and don't know, and, through retrieval, their knowledge is further strengthened. The retrieval memory test should require effort. It *should* be hard work.

This helps consolidate learning into a cohesive pattern in the brain; it also strengthens and multiplies the neural pathways so that the knowledge can be retrieved at a later date.

Increasing memory requires all of the steps outlined above. You need to encode the new material; you need to transfer it from short-term memory into long-term memory; and you must get it to 'adhere' in there securely. Then, use a method of association to help you retrieve the material at a later date. Information that has significance for you – or that is retrieved regularly – will stay in your memory for longer.

Donald Hebb, a Canadian neuropsychologist who studied how the neurons in the brain contribute to learning, has left us a legacy known as Hebb's Law: 'Neurons that fire together, wire together.' An example of this type of learning is the string of numbers that you use regularly, such as pin numbers and phone numbers. The more you retrieve them, the more you remember them. Similarly, lines of poetry you learned as a child, and recited regularly, can sometimes be easily recalled decades later. In short, the more you read, hear and recall information, the more that information is hardwired in your brain. Retrieval makes the neurons fire together and thus helps to wire them together.

It also seems that the more effort involved in retrieving, the more successful you will be: students need to incorporate retrieval exercises such as self-testing and quizzes into their day-to-day studies. Ideally they should space out the testing exercises by coming back to them the following day, so that they have to work hard to retrieve the information. Then, they should leave it for a day or two, or even a week, and test themselves again on the same material. This type of exercise will help the student to dispel the notion that they 'know' a subject just because they have been reading and rereading it. Self-testing and quizzing are extremely powerful tools for learning and remembering. Although self-testing can be very unappealing for the student (because it requires more effort than reading), it is definitely a better study strategy to adopt, and it makes better use of the student's time.

Remember the Greek philosopher Aristotle's famous quote: 'Exercise in repeatedly recalling a thing strengthens the memory.'

Other Techniques

A few other techniques have also been shown to help:

- *Mix up your revision and self-testing:* Many students focus single-mindedly on one subject and cram information, in the hope that they have really learned the subject material thoroughly. In fact, focusing solely on one subject is not the most effective way to study. Changing subjects and leaving intervals between testing and retesting sessions allows time to make the memory stronger. The more effort that is expended in remembering the information, the more entrenched the memory will become. Easier is definitely not better.
- *Feedback:* Feedback from others on incorrect answers also seems to increase memory and learning better than carrying out self-testing alone. With feedback, knowledge becomes more durable and deeply entrenched, possibly due to the emotional aspect of feedback. The more practical or emotional importance that knowledge has for you, the better you will retain it in your memory.
- *Teaching others:* Research suggests that you learn better when you have to teach the material to someone else. In fact, teaching someone else will mutually benefit both parties.
- *Handwriting notes and reading paper books:* Research also suggests that handwriting notes during a class or lecture helps you to remember better than if you type the notes on a laptop. Students who type tend to transcribe what has been said, whereas those who write longhand have to process the information as well as write it down. This seems to lead to better long-term comprehension. A similar phenomenon seems to occur with reading. Researchers have compared reading paper books and e-books. They found that students reading paper books had better comprehension of what they read and remembered it better. It seems that the tactile experience of reading a book aids the process of constructing a mental representation of the text and so aids memory and understanding.
- *Problems that are too advanced:* Oddly enough, attempting to solve a problem that is outside your current ability – a problem that requires knowledge you haven't come across yet – stretches your brain and helps it grow. It helps you to develop problem-solving skills and also to differentiate between different patterns of problems.

- *Sleep:* Memory is also enhanced by sleep. Much of that vast memory consolidation occurs during sleep. By sleeping in between self-testing/quizzing practice periods, you are giving yourself the best chance of embedding learning.

- *Exercise:* Taking regular exercise also increases a person's ability to remember (see Chapter 11).

- *Mental rehearsal:* Mentally rehearsing yourself remembering the subject studied easily and calmly before you fall asleep can also help to increase retention (see Chapter 12).

- *Reflection:* Reflecting on what you have studied and learned, and reflecting on your own performance, is an advanced skill, and leads to deeper learning. When you are reflecting, you are retrieving knowledge and earlier experiences from your memory. You are connecting these experiences to new experiences, and then visualising what you might do differently next time. Reflection is a form of retrieval practice: 'What happened?', 'How did I do?', 'What would I do differently next time to improve?'

- *Forgetting:* Sometimes you need to forget an old skill in order to learn a new one. For example, you may need to forget how to play tennis if you take up badminton or squash. Or you may need to forget words used in Spanish in order to learn the words in French. But it is important to remember that whatever Spanish words you have learned earlier will not have been forgotten completely. They can be easily picked up again later after a period of disuse. It is not the knowledge that is forgotten; rather, it is the cues needed in order to retrieve it.

When it comes to learning, you need to use all your senses – create pictures or drawings, use mnemonics or rhymes – as well as practical examples of what you want to remember. Everyone uses a number of different learning approaches, and using a mixture of techniques really enhances the triggers for remembering information. If your teenager uses all of these methods, it will go a long way towards increasing their memory and will enable them to use their study time effectively, so that they gain the most from their study time and do not waste it on ineffective methods.

While these strategies may seem mechanical and lacking in creativity, what is important to remember is that before anyone can be truly creative they need to embed the basic knowledge of the subject. Only then will they have the depth of knowledge to draw on to exercise their creative thinking and problem-solving skills. Without this basic knowledge, creativity is not based on solid foundations.

Remember that we also know that expert performance and ability are achieved as a result of hours of practice, and it is through this sustained effort that we accumulate the experience to discern wisely and respond appropriately in a given situation. Unfortunately, there are no shortcuts.

14

TEENAGERS AND RELATIONSHIPS, ROMANCE AND SEX

One of our most fundamental emotional needs is attention, and a primary way of ensuring this need is met is through friendship and intimacy. Finding and bonding with a mate, and creating a family, is one of our most basic instincts. One of the early indicators of adolescence is a new-found sexual interest in others.

LOVE AND ROMANCE

First and foremost, love is an emotion like any other – a temporary state that takes over our mind and our thinking. Like all positive emotions, it is extraordinarily pleasant. But, as you will recall from earlier chapters, meeting any need will make us feel good. In that sense, attention and connection – and love – are no different. However, what is different about love is that it expands our awareness of our surroundings and of ourselves. The boundaries between us and others recede. We feel open, and we see others more clearly and compassionately. This gives us a sense of connection – and can meet our need for meaning and purpose – of being part of something bigger than ourselves. Over time, the feeling of 'being in love' begins to subside. We do not stay in this heady state long-term, as is the case with any emotion.

First Love and Teenagers

For most teenagers, their first love is an unparalleled experience: nothing comes close to it in terms of intensity, excitement, obsession and positive feelings. The needs that are met through this first, romantic, requited love are many, which may be why it is so intoxicating.

The first important need that is met is giving and receiving attention – an experience that is hugely satisfying and can be even mesmerising. For a teenager, having someone with whom they are totally open (and who is equally open with them) creates a strong bond and a level of intimacy that they might not have experienced previously outside their immediate family. The teenage couple may share things they have never shared with another person, and they will be intensely concerned with each other's well-being. From the teenager's perspective, they have now found someone who completely understands them and accepts them for who they are.

There are many advantages associated with this intense experience of love at this age. The experience of being 'in love' refocuses a teenager's attention away from themselves onto another. The romantic relationship enables them to learn trust and compassion. It gives them the opportunity to expand their social circle as they are now exposed to the friends of their boyfriend or girlfriend. They have also gained an intimate best friend, one who accepts them and meets their need for friendship and intimacy. It changes how they view themselves. They now have someone they admire and who admires them and this gives them the sense that they are an admirable and good person.

So, when a teenager first falls in love, it is completely understandable that their boyfriend/girlfriend becomes the focal point of their life. They organise their life around that person – when they are with that person their need for attention, friendship and intimacy is met and they feel desirable, cared for and appreciated. Of course, most adults know that, by and large, the experiences of first love unfortunately do not last – even though the teenagers who are caught in this mesmerising state truly believe it will. If you suggest that this love is temporary, your teenager will almost certainly get very defensive, and will consider it patronising or demeaning. It may even elicit an angry reaction. So beware! Much as you might wish to give your teenager the benefit of your life experience, the risk is that anything negative you may say will come across as belittling of their intensely personal experience. They don't necessarily have the ability to understand that you too have probably fallen in love at various stages in your life, and that you probably know more about the subject of love and intimate relationships than they do.

This is the time to take a step back and be supportive, in order to preserve your relationship with your teenager, while simultaneously knowing that their romantic relationship will most likely run its course and peter out before long. Advice about stepping back and being non-judgemental is, of course, easy to dispense from afar; things may not be quite that easy in cases where, from the involved parent's point of view, the 'beloved' is not quite as fantastic as the teenage son or daughter believes them to be. Asking them how their friends see their new boy-friend or girlfriend can get them to think a bit more objectively about the other person. Overall, perhaps learning to bite your tongue and allow the relationship to run its course would be better at this point (assuming they are safe and the relationship is not abusive). Remember, this is your teenager's first experience of romantic love. They have no other experience to draw on at this time, and it is all the more exciting because it is new and unfamiliar territory.

Break-Ups

When first love comes to an end, it can be very traumatic for any adolescent, especially if they didn't want the romantic relationship to end. For most teenagers, the crisis will be short-lived, but while they are in the middle of the crisis it will dominate their lives and it will seem like their world has come to an end. In order for your teenage son or daughter to survive and readjust after a break-up – irrespective of whether they were the initiator or not – they will need to reorganise their social life and get back to spending more time with their other friends. This may be difficult, particularly if the romantic relationship was so intense that they focused much of their time and attention on their romantic partner and lost touch with their friends. When this happens to a teenager and they are completely distraught and it feels like they going through a huge crisis, just hang in there with them. In most cases, they will revert to being themselves within a month or so. What they need is gentle and quiet support from you and your family. They may not need nor want to discuss the relationship but, be assured, they will need your quiet understanding and compassionate, non-judgemental acceptance.

Some break-ups can re-evoke deeper losses that the teenager may have experienced in the past (such as the death of a close friend or a family member, a divorce, or a real or perceived abandonment by a parent). They may need professional help to deal with these events and become fully engaged in their current life again, and not stuck in past traumas. (The rewind technique is a very effective method of dealing with this quickly and safely – see Chapter 18.)

SEX

Discussing sex can be uncomfortable and embarrassing for adults, not only because of their own self-consciousness, but also because of the very open, sexualised society in which we now live. It can be difficult to find the right balance between not discussing sex, ignoring it and hoping it will go away, and being too open about the subject and expecting your teenager to do likewise. Teenagers too can be hugely embarrassed by the idea of talking about sex with their parents. The best approach is to try to see sex as just another topic of conversation, another subject in their lives that you want to discuss with them. Try to convey to them the dangers and possible consequences of sex in the same way as you have discussed many other life challenges and possible pitfalls: not wearing a helmet while riding a bike, failing exams as a result of not studying, drinking too much alcohol, or getting into a brawl or a dangerous situation.

It is not a good idea to ignore the topic and the possible consequences of sex, and hope that your son or daughter's school or someone else will do it for you. Ideally, parents and teenagers would sit down and have a calm conversation about sex, with the parents both giving information and answering questions. But we don't live in an ideal world and, for parents and teenagers alike, sex is an emotionally fraught subject, which in turn makes it an awkward topic of conversation for everyone. However, you do need to talk to your teenager if they are to have a balanced perspective on sex. They need to be aware of your stance on sex. Parents play an important role in these conversations, so try not to let your own embarrassment get in the way of giving your teenager the information they need.

Emphasise the link between sex and relationships, and explain that sexual arousal and experimentation is a natural development in an emotionally intimate relationship. As teenagers share their hopes, dreams and fears with one another, they become closer and more intimate with their respective boyfriend/girlfriend, and so it is only natural for them to become more physically intimate with each other. Once we become physical with another person, nature pumps the 'love hormone' oxytocin into our brains, in order to cement the bond. Becoming physical early in a relationship causes this release of oxytocin, which helps us trust and bond with the other person. This gives us the feeling that we have a closer bond than is maybe the case, and it might not be appropriate. The old adage of taking time in a romance before getting physically intimate has now been proven as wisdom by modern science.

Because teenage bodies and brains are changing so much, they are frequently in a state of confusion and these sexual feelings and urges become powerful forces in their lives. The simple fact is that nature predisposes them to have sex, so as to reproduce and increase the population – just like other animal species on the planet. Such sexual feelings will complicate and disrupt teenagers' lives and throw them off course in ways they will never have experienced before. Remember, the reproductive instincts of the teenager's limbic system (emotional brain) and the logic of the neocortex (rational brain) will be pulling them in different directions. So it is really important that they have the reference point of a stable, balanced adult in the midst of all this confusion.

ASK YOURSELF

If you can, try to recollect what it was like for you when you first experienced sexual feelings and urges as a teenager. Were you left to figure this out on your own, or was there someone you could talk to, or get advice from? What did you need at the time?

Teenagers who are looking for information will go online, and the internet is awash with information about sex. Some of this information is not only highly questionable, it is also dangerous, as it can prey on the ignorance and innocence of young people. Relying on the internet as their only, or main, source of information on sex could leave your teenage son or daughter highly vulnerable and unprotected. It is important that you give them sound, balanced information in order to counteract misinformation and the overtly sexualised media they are exposed to. Increased exposure to sexual content on television serves only to glamorise sex and gives adolescents false messages. Sex is given much higher importance than the development of strong intimate relationships – a subject that has far less appeal for young people.

Sexual activity greatly increases between the ages of fifteen and seventeen, and the average age of first menstruation and puberty is continuing to decline. For these reasons alone, it is important that conversations about sex are instigated by parents, and that teenagers are made aware of risks they may be running. Having sex in the early teenage years not only brings with it the risk of unwanted pregnancy, but also the risk of sexually transmitted diseases and infections.

Remember sex can be a way of bolstering self-esteem in the short term. It can seem like an attractive option for a teenager who doesn't feel good about themselves. A sexual encounter can be exciting, conveying a powerful message that they are worthwhile and desirable, which is very appealing for a teenager who has an underlying feeling that they are unloved. It would be very difficult for such a teenager to say 'no' to sex because they will almost certainly believe that it will make them feel better about themselves.

What to Do

Take the Bull by the Horns!

Talk to your teenager. Over time, your embarrassment and awkwardness is likely to lessen, but if it does not, and if the process is proving really difficult for you, ask another adult or the teenager's older siblings to speak to them. Alternatively, find out what your teenager's school is doing with regard to relationships and sexual education; knowing what they have learned there will perhaps make it easier for you to continue the conversation with them.

The truth is that you have very little control over your teenager's sex life, and so, for the sake of reducing your own anxiety levels, it is probably a good idea not to assume anything about what they are up to. Some people don't become sexually active until their late teens or early twenties. It is worth remembering that while you may not know exactly what type of sexual activity (if any) they are engaged in, you can probably exert more influence than you realise, especially when it comes to health and safety. For example, you can initiate a conversation about relationships and pregnancy without asking directly if they are sexually active. One effective and non-threatening way to do this is to watch your teenager's favourite television shows or films with them, and use the situations the characters find themselves in as a way to discuss difficult topics. Indeed, one of the few positives of watching television soaps with a teenager is that these programmes often have dramatic storylines about sex, drinking, drugs, bullying, ethical dilemmas and so on, and give plenty of opportunity for discussion. Ask your teenager how they think they would feel – or what they think they would do – if they found themselves in the situation of the characters. This is a great way to open up a conversation and create an opportunity for you to listen to their views and for them to hear yours. During the conversation – when your teenager expresses their views about the characters' dilemmas, reactions and behaviours – you will be able to glean a lot about your child's opinions, and how they themselves might react in a sex-related situation.

Don't Make Assumptions

One of the most common mistakes that anxious parents make is assuming that their teens are already sexually active when perhaps they are not. So, tread carefully and make no assumptions. Inform them about what they need to know and encourage them to take their time and wait. Without appearing to lecture them, try to find a way to let them know that older teenagers often regret becoming sexually active early in life, and later wish that they had waited. This can be done by telling a story about another person (perhaps a relative or a friend), or by using a movie storyline or a novel/autobiography as a reference point.

The Difference between Physical and Emotional Intimacy

Talk to your teenagers about the difference between physical and emotional intimacy. This is important because some teenagers seek out physical intimacy (i.e. sex) in order to achieve emotional intimacy.

A good way to approach this is to have a general conversation about how we behave differently with close friends than we do with strangers and acquaintances and about the different levels of trust we have with these different groups. This may help them understand the importance of establishing real emotional intimacy and trust with a partner before becoming sexual, which may otherwise only serve to overly complicate the relationship.

Health

If you are concerned about your teenager's sexual health or if you suspect they are sexually active and need to consider birth control options, offer to take them to your GP or a family planning clinic. Teenagers can be haunted by sexual fears and worries that they dare not admit to you or their friends. These should be taken seriously and listened to non-judgementally by an adult and, where necessary, by a professional. If teenage pregnancy is an issue, it too needs to be handled with compassion and understanding. Blaming and shaming a teenager can have a silencing and paralysing effect on them, which is not going to help them make good decisions. Kindness and compassion will go further, keep your relationship intact, and preserve your teenager's dignity and sense of self.

SEXUAL ORIENTATION AND TRANSGENDER ISSUES

What should a parent do if their teenager is not heterosexual or if they are confused about their gender identity? What if they are lesbian, gay, bisexual or transgender (LGBT)? At the time of writing, several research studies show that at any given time between 5 and 10 per cent of the world's population is gay. Logically, therefore, the equivalent percentage of parents may find themselves having to deal with their son or daughter's sexual orientation. While the number of transgender people in society is smaller (current estimates are between 1 and 2 per cent), it is an issue that an increasing number of teenagers and parents are confronting. Research has shown that young people who are members of the LGBT community are much more likely to suffer from mental health problems. The onus is on us, the adults, to examine our own views on sexual orientation and gender identity, and deal with our reactions in a way that does not create additional distress for vulnerable LGBT youngsters.

If your teenager is aware that they are lesbian, gay, bisexual or transgender, it is likely that this fact – and issues related to it – will take up a lot of their thinking and be a dominant factor in their lives. The statistics on incidents of bullying and harassment of LGBT teenagers present quite a damning indictment of society and its attitude to sexual orientations and gender identities outside the norm. If we are to responsibly address the mental health of our children – irrespective of their sexual orientation/gender identity – we need to question our personal prejudices and make society safer, more compassionate and caring for all young people.

Acknowledging the Facts versus Hiding the Facts

Being gay, lesbian, bisexual or transgender still carries a social stigma in society and so many LGBT adolescents try to conceal the fact, fearing rejection. This disconnect between their true self and the self they show to the world can be confusing and threatening, and can create a lot of inner turmoil and rumination. Those who are aware of their sexual orientation/gender identity and are fearful of the consequences may even attempt to change their sexuality or conform to a gender identity that feels alien to them. Most likely, their greatest fear is that they will be rejected by friends and family. This deep fear of rejection and isolation places these teenagers in the highest risk category for mental health problems. The teenager needs to acknowledge and accept their own sexual orientation/gender identity. For some, this acknowledgement happens as early as their primary school years. For others, this does not happen until they reach adulthood; and some never acknowledge it at all – either to themselves or to their wider family, friends, colleagues or employers.

Carrying what is perceived as a shameful secret can have detrimental effects on any person's mental health. Secrets can gnaw at us and affect our self-esteem. Teenagers having such a secret may be consumed by a sense of dread – worrying what would happen if their secret was revealed. Unfortunately, many believe that the resulting prejudice against them would be extreme, and their anxiety may lead to self-loathing, self-harm and suicide. The figures speak for themselves:

4.2 per cent of heterosexual adolescents attempt suicide. The figure for gay and lesbian adolescents is 21 per cent and the figure for transgender adolescents is a staggering 41 per cent.

Some Final Thoughts and Reflections

Try to put yourself in an LGBT teenager's shoes for a moment. They are aware of something about themselves that some individuals in society may have told them is wrong or shameful. They may also believe that if their family knew the truth about their sexual orientation/gender identity, it could lead to complete rejection by them. This type of negativity is common in LGBT teenagers, and is often the result of either explicit or implicit views about homosexuality/trans identities expressed by the adults around them. Small wonder therefore that LGBT teenagers are so vulnerable to mental health problems.

Question your own prejudices and whether you may have passed on any negative views to your own teenage son or daughter. Also consider whether your prejudices have in any way affected LGBT individuals, or have influenced people who discriminate against LGBT individuals. All teenagers, irrespective of their sexual orientation/gender identity, need acceptance and nurturance. They also need groups of peers who accept and understand them, and who appreciate the issues faced by LGBT adolescents.

Teenagers are the next generation of adults. They are the individuals who will shape our communities in the future. Encouraging them to work for a fair and just society, where all individuals are respected equally, serves to help all of us evolve and become a more mature, civilised and respectful society that cherishes all its citizens.

Part IV

TEENAGER DIFFICULTIES

15

Teenagers and Stress

What Everyone Needs to Know about Stress

The term 'stress' was first coined in the 1950s by Hans Selye, who defined it as 'the non-specific response of the body to any demand for change'. He made a distinction between the terms 'distress' (which is what we now tend to call stress) and 'eustress' (or stretch, which is the stress or excitement we experience when confronted with a challenge we want to overcome).

Stress occurs when we feel threatened; when our emotional needs are not being met (see Chapter 2). You will most likely feel stressed if you believe you are under threat of some kind, for instance when you feel insecure. Examples might include:

- Being bullied at school, or facing the possibility of losing your job or home.
- When you feel your privacy is being invaded, when others have been reading your emails, text messages or letters.
- When you feel isolated or alone in the world.
- When you feel overwhelmed or 'out of control' because someone else is calling the shots.

When your needs are not being met, your brain triggers the stress response and pumps cortisol, epinephrine (adrenaline) and norepinephrine into your bloodstream. Once this happens, your heart rate increases, your blood pressure rises, your senses sharpen and a surge in glucose gives your muscles the energy needed to get moving – whether that is out of the path of an oncoming car or starting on a piece of work that is required for a particular deadline. Stress is your brain's way of giving you a burst of energy quickly; it is your body telling you what it is that you need to do.

You can also get stressed when something you are involved in is *not* stretching you. For example, a student who is bored with their work may become very stressed. The stress caused by the boredom may result in them trying to create something more 'interesting', causing disruption as they seek novelty and challenge.

THE TYPES OF STRESS

Eustress or Stretch

People are often surprised to learn that there is a positive side to stress and that it can act as a motivator, jolting your body into action in a positive way. If you didn't have some stress, you would end up bored and depressed, and not do anything. Eustress or being stretched is what you feel when you undertake a challenge that is stretching you, or when you are aiming to achieve a particular goal. For example, you experience eustress when you are about to perform, on stage or in a sport, and you are challenging yourself. Eustress, or being stretched, gets you to focus your attention when you have something important to do, like study for an exam, take on a challenge, or impress someone.

Increasingly, psychologists are investigating the positive aspects of being stretched. Several studies have found that being stretched can strengthen the immune system, increase resistance to infection, help protect against ageing and aid brain development. It can also help you to perform tasks more efficiently, improve memory and improve heart function. Therefore, far from being something that you need to eliminate, a certain amount of stretch stimulates and is good for you.

Distress or Stress

The other kind of stress is distress. Generally, this is what we normally mean when we use the term 'stress'. It is what you feel when you have either too many or too few challenges in life. Being bored can be just as stressful as being overwhelmed with too many demands. If stress hormones are coursing around your bloodstream over a long period, such as weeks or months, it begins to have a very negative effect, leading to exhaustion and depression. Once this tipping point has been reached, it can be difficult to get your problems under control, particularly as the stress hormones will also affect your thinking and you end up making unwise decisions.

Knowing the symptoms will help you to recognise when you are experiencing stress. Such symptoms may include an increased number of colds or aches and pains, foggy thinking, worsening of autoimmune diseases such as eczema and psoriasis, or an IBS (inflammatory bowel syndrome) flare-up.

How to Tell the Difference between Stretch and Stress

How can you tell the difference between situations that provide an opportunity to stretch yourself (which makes you resilient), and situations that generate long-term, chronic stress (which affects you negatively)? Table 1 provides a quick guide.

Table 1: The Difference between Stretch and Stress

Stretch	Stress
• Challenges feel as if they are within your control. Exams are a good example – the amount of study you do is under your control.	• The challenges feel out of your control. Situations where you feel helpless, trapped and out of control can create the most damaging type of stress.
• There is light at the end of the tunnel. You can see that the challenge will come to an end.	• There seems to be no end in sight. Situations are chronic and ongoing with no rest between deadlines or stressful events. An example might be a difficult boss, teacher or parent, or major financial problems or chronic illness, where there seems to be no solution.
• The challenge is followed by rest, allowing the body to recuperate.	• The stressful situation is not followed by rest. It is ongoing and chronic.

(Continued)

Table 1 (*Continued*)

Stretch	Stress
• Challenges are focused outwards, away from excessive thinking and rumination.	• Challenges are focused inwards on past mistakes or regrets, causing rumination and self-judgement.

STRESS – AN UNAVOIDABLE REALITY

Stress is an unavoidable reality. As we have seen, the goal is not the absence of stress – without it, life would become very dull. The trick is to become aware of the tipping point where it moves from a feeling of dealing with an exciting and stretching challenge to a feeling of being overwhelmed and out of control.

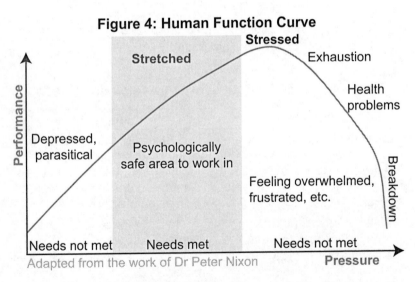

Figure 4: Human Function Curve

Adapted from the work of Dr Peter Nixon

As you can see from Figure 4, too much or too little pressure results in difficulties. Being aware of this can help you to take action, using small, achievable steps that enable you to bring yourself back into equilibrium.

So, what is happening to your body when you get stressed? What is happening inside your brain, and how can you manage this better? The first thing to know is that when you feel stressed it is because your *emotional brain* has taken control of your physical and mental responses. It has hijacked your *thinking (rational) brain* (see Chapter 1). If you understand the physical makeup of the brain and the roles played by the different parts, it can help you manage your stress levels better. What follows will give you some idea of how these various parts interact with each other.

All inputs to the brain (excluding smell) are initially sent to an area known as the thalamus, which acts like a switchboard of information. It directs the signals simultaneously to the amygdala and the neocortex. The amygdala is a small, almond-shaped region of the brain whose job it is to monitor the environment for threat. The neocortex is the most developed part of the brain, and is responsible for our thinking. The amygdala will receive the information signal in about a tenth of the time it takes for the same signal to be received by the neocortex; therefore the amygdala will be the first part of the brain to react. The amygdala is a very basic, primitive part of the brain that evaluates all incoming stimuli in a very simplistic manner. It does this by searching for an appropriate pattern-match and, depending on what it locates, determining if there is a potential threat or not. Remember the APET model:

A	P	E	T
Activating agent	Pattern-match	Emotion	Thought

If a pattern-match to a previous threatening experience is created (for example, severe turbulence on a flight), signals are sent to the pituitary gland to flood your body with stress hormones. You are now in the 'fight or flight' state of stress and the amygdala's perception of the severity of the threat will be matched by the volume of cortisol it secretes. As you will know from your own experience of stressful situations in the past (severe turbulence, a car accident or someone screaming at you), your physical reaction to the event happens in nanoseconds – so fast that you are completely unconscious of the steps involved in the process. And it all happens well before you have had time to think rationally about whatever it was that triggered your reaction.

One of the effects of cortisol is that it causes the neural connections between the emotional (mammalian) brain and the thinking (neocortex) brain to begin to close down. While that may seem odd, there is a very good reason for this from an evolutionary point of view. Imagine our prehistoric ancestor, out in the savannah minding his own business, when he finds his path blocked by a lion. In such threatening circumstances, it made perfect sense that within nanoseconds the muscles in his body were flooded with cortisol, which propelled him into a state of 'fight or flight'. If he chose the 'flight' option (as opposed to 'fight'), he would have headed for the nearest escape route as fast as his legs could carry him. If, instead of running away, our man had stopped to *think* about his situation (i.e. weighed up his options), it probably would have resulted in the lion attacking him and, inevitably, death. Far wiser for our man to get out of the lion's way as fast as possible, retreat to a safe place, and *then* consider what to do next.

STRESS AND THE MODERN MAN, WOMAN OR TEENAGER

Like our prehistoric ancestor who survived mauling by the lion by putting his energy into a *physical response* to the threat, as soon as a threat to twenty-first-century man, woman or teenager has passed and the level of cortisol in the brain has subsided, the normal functioning of the brain can resume, the neural connections can open up and, once again, the person can access their thinking (rational) brain. This explains why, when we are very stressed, we literally cannot think straight.

It is also why we often regret the decisions we made when we were extremely stressed – a time when we did not have access to all of our intelligence. We are much better off, therefore, to wait until we are calm before making important decisions. This also explains the common scenario of the student who goes blank in an exam. Excess cortisol cuts off access to their thinking brain and, try as they might, they cannot access the information they have retained in their memory. This experience causes more stress and the subsequent release of more cortisol, which just makes matters worse.

One of the other effects of cortisol is that it speeds up your heart rate, breathing and metabolism, and also increases your blood pressure. These physical changes will enable you to react quickly and effectively to handle the pressure of the moment. But cortisol also affects the physiology of your body, contributing to those uncomfortable feelings associated with stress: a knot in your stomach, diarrhoea, frequent urination, skin rashes, etc.

STRESS AND GENDER

How you respond to stress will be determined by a number of factors, one of which is gender. Recent research shows that the female stress response differs from that of the male response. In prehistoric times, our survival depended on being able to respond effectively to a threat. For a male, the 'fight or flight' response mentioned above makes sense, but for a female, her survival and that of her children was better served by being part of a group of other females (while the men went off to hunt). For a female, fighting would not have been a good option; fleeing with her children in tow would not have served her well, either. Her best option by far was to tend to her children and maintain strong friendships with other females, something that modern scientists describe as the 'tend and befriend' female stress response.

'Tend and befriend' explains the instinctive need that most females have to talk at length with their friends as a means of reducing their stress levels. By talking, communicating and bonding with others, our levels of cortisol reduce. The next time you become aware of your teenage daughter's need to communicate constantly with her friends, this insight into her stress response may help you understand the biological drives behind her behaviour.

TEENAGERS AND STRESS

So, what about teenagers and stress? Recent research findings show that the average teenager secretes more cortisol and adrenaline in their day-to-day lives than either children or adults. The reason for this is due to two key factors – the brain structure of a teenager and the hormonal changes they are going through. These two factors contribute to teenagers' difficulty in regulating their emotional reactions. Knowing this may help you to be more tolerant of them and also help them reduce their stress so that they can think more clearly and behave more appropriately.

The onset of puberty automatically increases the cortisol level sharply, and it remains elevated into young adulthood and up to the mid-twenties. Cortisol can help the body prepare to deal with stressors. Too much cortisol, however, is associated with numerous negative outcomes, including increased vulnerability to depression and anxiety, increased hyper-vigilance, weakened immune response and a generally overwhelmed, exhausted and 'freaked out' feeling. The stress response is not only *stronger* in adolescents than in adults, it also stays activated for *longer*, which explains why an agitated teenager is likely to go completely over the top if you suggest that they calm down. Teenagers don't have it easy; when they get stressed they experience it far more strongly than any adult.

TOOLS FOR MANAGING STRESS

There is no doubt that life in general is stressful, and that living with teenagers going through change and turmoil can add greatly to an already stressful life. You may be simultaneously dealing with work-related stress, financial worries, ageing parents, relationship problems and/or younger children. Consequently, how can you best help yourself to cope better with stress and help your teenagers to do likewise?

Stress affects thinking and decision-making, memory, concentration, sleep and the ability to enjoy life, but it can be managed if you have the right information and knowledge, and if you practise the skills of stress reduction. If you find managing stress difficult, it will really pay dividends in the long run for both you and your teenager if you put time and effort into developing these skills. Making the decision to learn these skills can mark the first step in really taking charge of your own emotions.

There are many ways you can go about helping yourself to manage stress, but what is important is that you choose a method that works for you: we are all different, and what works for one person might not work for another. Stress reduction and relaxation can be achieved in many ways – through exercise, meditation, reading, music, gardening, hobbies and other activities that take your attention away from whatever is causing you stress and allow you to become absorbed in something totally different. Relaxation gives your brain a chance to focus attention on something other than your worries; it gives your mind a rest. Therefore, creating a schedule in your life that includes some 'downtime' can really make a difference.

Sleep is one obvious time when you completely switch off and relax. The importance and benefits of getting good-quality, restful sleep are outlined in Chapter 12. The benefits of regular exercise and good nutrition as an antidote to stress have also been outlined in Chapter 11. Apart from meeting these needs, what other actions are useful?

What You Can Do for Yourself

These tips apply equally to parents and teenagers, in fact to everyone who experiences stress.

- Review your life so as to increase your resources and resilience, e.g. eating habits, sleep, exercise, work, friends and hobbies.
- Set positive, realistic and achievable goals that meet your needs and do not overwhelm you.
- Ask yourself: 'What can I do to help myself?' Often, there are small actions you can take that will help you feel more in control. You can use the Emotional Needs Audit at the end of this chapter to assist you in doing this.
- Take time to visit friends and family, and get support, particularly for women and girls.
- Take up a hobby or a sport that gets you involved with your community and takes you away from the source of the stress. Give your brain some 'time out' to switch off.
- Set a time limit on the stressful situation and promise yourself that you will take some action when this point is reached. For example, say: 'If there is no change by the end of the year, I will quit the team/job/course, etc.' Providing yourself with an 'out' can give you a sense of control that will help you deal with the situation better. You are creating an 'end in sight', which will help you cope better.
- Change your attitude. Remember that what often determines whether or not a situation is stretching or overwhelming is your own attitude to it. See if you can frame the situation differently, perhaps as a challenge that you will learn from.
- Monitor your self-talk. Try to observe how you speak to yourself. Are you overly critical of yourself? Do you speak to yourself in a way that you would never speak to another person? Try to be kinder and more compassionate to yourself.
- Observe your thought patterns. Ask yourself how you approach difficult situations or challenges. Are you overly negative? Do you see yourself as having 'fixed' abilities? Do you say to yourself, 'I could never do that', or 'I'm not good enough'? Or do you wonder if you *can* do something and give it a go, even though you may not feel confident?

- Think of past successes and believe in yourself.
- Take one small step at a time and give yourself the experience of success. This will motivate you to take another step.
- If you realise that your expectations of yourself are very high, reduce them. Do not try to achieve perfection, it is not possible. All that can be expected of any of us is that we do our best.
- Be good to yourself and congratulate yourself for each step you have taken and for each achievement, however small. Only then prepare yourself for the next step and stay focused only on that one. You will be less likely to get overwhelmed if you break the task down into steps and just focus on each step.
- Take time out of your life to do something playful or quiet. Build in rest and recuperation times; ensure you have time for relaxation.
- Introduce more fun and laughter into your life, it really does act like a tonic and can help to relieve stress.
- Get professional help: take a stress management class. Go to your GP or see a good counsellor. Learn from others how to manage stress.

The Art of Reframing

All kinds of stressful situations can occur on a regular basis – bad weather, traffic jams, strikes, a child suddenly becoming ill, exams – none of which you can control. What you can do, however, is choose a number of typical, stressful situations and use them to learn the art of reframing. By this I mean practise with these everyday scenarios and use them to reframe your perception of them to create a more positive attitude. This will help you to deal with actual stressful situations in the future. Essentially, this can act like training and a rehearsal for the major – and much more difficult – life events that inevitably happen to all of us.

Reframing involves creating a positive frame for a perceived negative experience. So, say for example your car breaks down, useful reframes might include:

- 'It gives me an opportunity to get exercise and to walk or use public transport, which is a more environmentally friendly and economic way of travelling.'

- 'The fact that the car broke down means that it may have prevented us from having an accident in the future. Now that the car is repaired, we will be safer.'

Or if you get a poor mark in an exam:

- 'I thought I was better at that subject, but now I know what I need to concentrate on so that I do better next time.'
- 'Perhaps I need to get some extra help in that subject as I have always struggled with it and I need it to get into my preferred college course.'

As well as the therapeutic value to your mental health that may be derived from practising reframing, the exercise of finding a silver lining in every cloud is fun. Moreover, by practising with smaller challenges, you can build your 'reframing muscle' and this will mean that you will have an increased ability to reframe when confronted with the more serious challenges of life.

Hobbies and 'Flow'

Why does having an absorbing hobby or activity make a difference? You may already know something about the concept of 'flow', which was first described by the Hungarian psychologist Mihaly Csikszentmihalyi in his book *Flow*.

'Flow' is a state of absorbed concentration on an activity to such an extent that the person is so totally focused on the activity that nothing else seems to matter. It has been likened to the feeling that sportspeople describe as 'being in the zone'. If you have ever been so involved in some activity that it seemed time passed really quickly and you were almost completely unaware of everything going on around you, then you were probably in a state of 'flow'. People who are involved in a creative activity such as painting, drawing, writing, gardening or playing a musical instrument will all have had this experience, and it is a very positive state to be in. Obviously, you cannot be in this state all the time, but periods of time in this state can really rejuvenate your brain and allow you to switch off from your worries. Finding an activity in which you can experience this 'flow' can therefore be hugely beneficial in terms of managing stress.

7/11 Breathing

Other ways of helping yourself get into a relaxed state include various breathing techniques such as 7/11 breathing. This is a very simple breathing technique that can really help to calm your emotional brain, even when you are stressed or anxious. Remember that when you are stressed, your breathing quickens in order to inhale as much oxygen as possible for the anticipated action we are about to take. This is an automatic, instinctive reaction. Therefore, when you change your breathing so that the *exhaled* breath is longer than the *inhaled* breath, you interrupt the automatic, quick, shallow breathing that inevitably kicks in. This is how to do 7/11 breathing:

- Inhale deep into your lungs as if you were breathing into your stomach. Keep your shoulders and your body relaxed so that only your stomach moves, like a balloon expanding. Inhale like this for a count of seven.
- Then, slowly exhale as much air as you can, as if the balloon was deflating. Do this for a count of eleven. If you run out of air, just continue breathing out until you reach the count of eleven before taking your next breath.

The mechanism of 7/11 breathing works like this: inhalation triggers the sympathetic nervous system (arousal) and stresses the body slightly, whereas exhalation stimulates the parasympathetic nervous system (the relaxation response) and gives the message to your brain that you can relax and calm down. Think of what you do when you have completed a stressful event, such as an exam. Once outside the exam hall, you breathe out a huge sigh of relief, i.e. a long outbreath, and you relax. 7/11 breathing also mimics the breathing you do when you are at your most relaxed, i.e. when you sleep. Breathing out more slowly than breathing in ensures that the relaxation response counteracts and reduces the stress response.

7/11 breathing is a very powerful technique, which can, if used properly, stop a panic attack. Regularly practising this type of breathing

– even when you are not stressed – will help you develop an ability to calm yourself when you are stressed, and strengthen your confidence that you *can* calm yourself effectively by using this method.

Training Your Breathing to Help You Relax

Other methods for training your breathing to help you relax include swimming, jogging or other sports that require you to breathe out slowly. Swimming strokes where you inhale and then exhale slowly will help you train your breathing. Jogging is another exercise that will help you learn how to breathe properly. In addition, these activities deliver all the other advantages of exercise that will help you reduce your stress.

Playing a wind instrument, such as the flute, will also teach you to take in a short breath and elongate your exhaled breath. Similarly, if you sing, you have to breathe in the same way – singing with long, exhaled breaths. These activities all help you to indirectly learn to manage your breathing and focus on your relaxing, exhaled breath. Playing a sport, singing or playing an instrument are all the more beneficial if they are carried out with other people; such activities can also be a way of getting your emotional needs for friendship and community met at the same time.

Progressive Muscle Relaxation

You could also try what is known as progressive muscle relaxation. It works as follows. Pick a part of your body to start with, it could be your hands, shoulders, feet or wherever. Now clench all the muscles there as hard as you can. It sometimes helps to observe them while you are doing this. Concentrate on tensing the muscles and the physical sensations you feel there. Some people like to close their eyes so that they can concentrate better on these sensations.

Now, while concentrating on the physical sensations, slowly release the muscles and notice the change from tension to relaxation. Allow that feeling of relaxation to spread all over your body. You can repeat the cycle again on the same muscles and focus on how your body relaxes more and more each time you do it.

Mindfulness

Mindfulness, meditation and journaling (keeping a daily diary) are also popular ways of managing stress levels, but such activities are not for everyone, as sometimes sitting still and observing or writing down your thoughts only serves to increase your stress levels. If this is the case for you, start by using the 7/11 breathing technique described above to calm yourself, and then you can start to meditate. If you find that you can calm your mind using mindfulness, meditation and journaling, these can be very effective.

A guided meditation may work better for some people because this type of relaxation requires you to focus on someone else's voice and follow their lead, which can help you avoid getting caught up in your own stressful thoughts. Advice and information on mindfulness and meditation techniques are readily available online.

Guided Visualisation

You can create your own guided visualisation by using your imagination. This is easily done, and if it helps you could record your own voice. All you need to do is imagine yourself in a beautiful, safe place in nature – one where you would choose to spend some relaxing time if you had the opportunity. It could be a beach, a forest, somewhere in the mountains, or a beautiful garden – it doesn't matter where it is located, or even if it's real, just as long as it is somewhere you associate with relaxation.

- Start by finding yourself somewhere comfortable to sit or lie down, and close your eyes. Relax all the muscles in your body as much as you can, and imagine yourself setting out to spend some time in this beautiful place. Focus on all the details – the colour of the sea, the trees, the grass, the flowers. Focus on the sounds you can hear, the smells, the feel of this place, whether it is the sand under your feet or the clear mountain air. Just immerse yourself as much as you can in this beautiful place and allow yourself to relax and have some 'downtime'.
- Once you are fully immersed in this place, imagine the changes you would like to see happen in your life. For example, perhaps

you can imagine yourself managing your stress better if you take more exercise, join a class or try a new hobby. You can use this time to imagine the good changes you would like to make in your life. Sometimes when we are in this relaxed state we can see new solutions to whatever is stressing us. When you feel ready, slowly bring yourself back to reality.

You may be amazed at how refreshed you feel after using this technique even for a short while. Guided visualisation is also a great way to help yourself fall asleep easily, or to fall back asleep should you wake up in the middle of the night.

Laughter

And then there is laughter, 'the best medicine'. Watching your favourite comedy sketch, television show or film can take you out of yourself and away from your worries, and give your brain a break from rumination. Alternatively, if you have the opportunity, spend an evening at a comedy club with a friend and immerse yourself in laughter, or just spend time in the company of a good friend, swapping stories and reminiscing about funny incidents in your past.

BUILDING RESILIENCE

Resilience is not built by avoiding stress, it is built by developing the ability to regulate and utilise the natural stress response so that it works for you and not against you. Building resilience involves mastering the techniques outlined above along with ensuring that your emotional needs are met in balance. Do an Emotional Needs Audit (see p. 144) on yourself and check if your needs are being met in balance. Research has shown that when your emotional needs are met, you can cope better, recover better from adversity and develop and grow from difficult experiences. Check out your own life and see if you have enough friends, a supportive community, stretching and challenging goals, time out for yourself, recognition for your achievements, and a sense of control and security. If you find that some of these areas are lacking, you now have a framework to help you create a more satisfying life.

The Emotional Needs Audit

How well are <u>your</u> innate emotional needs being met?

Nature has programmed all of us with physical and emotional needs. These are the 'human givens' that cannot be avoided. How stressed we are depends on how well they are being met now, and how well we deal with the situation when they are not. Rate, in your judgement, how well the following emotional needs are being met in your life now, on a scale of one to seven (where 1 means not met at all, and 7 means being very well met), by ticking the appropriate boxes.

Question	NO	SOMETIMES	YES
Do you feel secure in all major areas of your life (such as your home, work, environment)?	1 2 3 4 5 6 7
Do you feel you receive enough attention?	1 2 3 4 5 6 7
Do you think you give other people enough attention?	1 2 3 4 5 6 7
Do you feel in control of your life most of the time?	1 2 3 4 5 6 7
Do you feel part of the wider community?	1 2 3 4 5 6 7
Can you obtain privacy when you need to?	1 2 3 4 5 6 7
Do you have an intimate relationship in your life (one where you are totally physically and emotionally accepted for who you are by at least one person, this could be a close friend)?	1 2 3 4 5 6 7
Do you feel an emotional connection to others?	1 2 3 4 5 6 7
Do you feel you have status that is acknowledged?	1 2 3 4 5 6 7
Are you achieving things and competent in at least one major area of your life?	1 2 3 4 5 6 7
Are you mentally and/or physically stretched in ways which give you a sense of meaning and purpose?	1 2 3 4 5 6 7

- If your scores are mostly low, you are more likely to be suffering stress symptoms.
- If any need is scored 3 or less this is likely to be a major stressor for you.
- Even if only one need is marked very low it can be enough of a problem to seriously affect your mental and emotional stability.

Stress, anxiety, anger, depression and addiction are the result of our innate needs not being met, either due to environmental factors, harmful conditioning or a misuse of imagination (worrying). People do not have mental health problems when their innate needs are being met in balanced, healthy ways. By highlighting areas in your life where your essential needs aren't being met as well as they could be, you can use this questionnaire to help you think constructively about how your life could be improved.

16

TEENAGERS AND TANTRUMS

Roaring, shouting, slamming doors and generally throwing tantrums are often hallmarks of the teenage years. But what is it that prompts teenagers (and us) to suddenly get so wound up and aggressive? Why do we all say things in the heat of the moment that we really don't mean and regret afterwards?

The purpose of anger is to defend us from harm when we perceive that we are under threat. When we get angry we choose the 'fight' rather than the 'flight' response. The decision to fight rather than run away is made following an instantaneous, unconscious assessment of the situation. We express anger, either verbally or physically, if we perceive that we can win.

When we get angry, we experience certain physiological responses, as extra adrenaline, cortisol and glucose are pumped into our bloodstream. Our breathing becomes faster, our blood pressure rises, and males get a surge of testosterone. All this means that we lose the ability to think clearly and make sensible decisions. We are emotionally hijacked and lose any connection with our rational, complex brain. We are so focused on the threat that we actually hear less and lose our peripheral vision. Extreme anger changes our thinking, causing us to think in the 'kill or be killed' mode of the 'fight or flight' response.

The upside to this is that anger allows us to dedicate all our energy to standing our ground and fighting. If we didn't have this ability, we would be defenceless and very vulnerable. The other positive of anger is that it allows us to recognise, and respond to, unjust situations. Throughout history, anger has motivated people to work for a more just society, to change laws and to stand up to aggression and protect vulnerable people. Anger has been the fuel behind revolutions, equal rights, child protection legislation and many other humanitarian and civilising changes. It is good to appreciate how useful anger can be when it is managed and utilised in a positive way. Unfortunately, many of us were not taught the necessary skills to manage anger in a healthy way. Indeed, depending on how you were brought up, your angry outbursts may have been punished, ignored or rewarded. As a consequence, all of us are programmed to deal with anger in different ways.

Excessive anger poses a serious health risk for the angry person. Where angry outbursts are continual or frequent, the effect of being constantly flooded by cortisol has been shown to have long-term adverse health effects. It depresses the immune system and we become much more prone to viruses and bacteria when we are constantly angry.

Anger can lead to bullying and we may take out our anger on others whom we perceive to be a threat or weaker than us in some way. It can lead to accidents and mistakes because it is difficult to think clearly when we are angry. Anger can also progress into violence; this is especially true of younger people who do not have the same control over their emotions. This can be exacerbated by hormonal changes and the neuronal changes happening in their brains.

GENDER DIFFERENCES

Most people believe that excessive anger is more of a male than a female phenomenon; this is not actually the case. It's just that there is a difference in how each gender expresses its anger; make no mistake, a teenage girl's rage can be quite ferocious.

When males get angry, they experience a rush of testosterone, which fuels the urge to fight, and this can make it more difficult for them to manage their anger. Girls, on the other hand, are better at controlling their anger for longer, but are also much better at bearing grudges, which they will sometimes hold on to for years. It is important for both sexes to understand their own destructive expressions of anger, and learn to let go of angry thoughts and impulses.

WHAT HELPS AND WHAT HINDERS?

Certain physiological and psychological conditions can make it more difficult to control anger outbursts. For instance, any condition that affects the brain, such as stroke or dementia, will impair a person's ability to manage their anger. Individuals diagnosed on the autistic spectrum can feel huge frustration and have difficulty remaining calm.

Any significant changes in our physical bodies can reduce our ability to manage any of our emotions, including anger. Such changes range from physical illness to tiredness, hunger, hormonal fluctuations/treatment and pain (either chronic or acute). Drugs that reduce our inhibitions (alcohol, for example) or any kind of addictive cravings (such as nicotine, alcohol, drugs, sex or sugar) all reduce our ability to stay in control of our anger impulses.

Teenagers are particularly prone to angry outbursts due to all the changes they are undergoing, and when they let their anger get out of control it can cause psychological trauma as well as physical injury or violence. Talking about and expressing anger doesn't always help, although it is often suggested as a healthy thing to do. Talking about what is making you angry can sometimes make you *more* angry, not less. Excessively rehashing the issue will only serve to make you feel worse. By churning the event over and over you are continuously making yourself angry. However, finding someone who will listen to you, hear your point of view, help you put it in perspective and help you see the problem in a different light by reframing it can really help you calm down and let your anger subside.

SOME OF THE FACTORS THAT CONTRIBUTE TO EXCESSIVE ANGER

Build-Up of Stress

Whenever we have too many demands on our time and our energy, and we become too stressed, a relatively minor event or an additional burden may serve as the last straw. As a result, we may blow our top at an innocent bystander, and afterwards we may regret the outburst. If your anger is directed at a child, then a good way to handle this is to apologise to them and let them know they didn't deserve to be spoken to in that way. Your child will learn from you the importance of taking responsibility for our own behaviour.

Anger, rows and tantrums often seem to be confined to our families and it can be infuriating that our teenagers behave so politely and courteously to those outside the family. It is the same with parents – we really love our children and we want to help them, so when they seem to be going down a destructive road, or messing up their lives in some way, we get angry to try to get them to change. Because we have an emotional investment in our families we have higher expectations of them and when they do not live up to our expectations we can get frustrated and end up nagging and making matters worse. Add to this the fact that we often treat family members with less respect than we would outsiders; we may take things for granted and invade each other's privacy. This type of behaviour can really irritate, and our patience and tolerance is limited.

Lacking Skills to Negotiate or Manage Anger

We all learn behaviour through seeing what works and, unfortunately, some people have learned that getting angry works as a way of getting their needs met. Others may have learned that emotional blackmail or other strategies (such as sulking, giving the cold shoulder, faking illness or damaging reputations or belongings) enable them to meet their needs. Some adults and teenagers haven't been exposed to the skills of anger management and negotiation, and need to actively learn these skills. Interestingly, this is now recognised as a major problem in China, where people who grew up being doted on and indulged as the only child did not have the opportunity to develop anger management and negotiation skills through interaction with their siblings – an unfortunate consequence of China's one-child policy.

Low Self-Esteem

If someone has low self-esteem, and has been made to feel worthless or inadequate, they may get angry easily, as they interpret remarks by others as criticisms. Someone who is insecure can be very sensitive and can take things personally when nothing malicious was intended.

This can lead to incorrect interpretations and angry reactions, or even angry rumination, which may further fuel their anger.

Too High Self-Esteem

On the other hand, if someone thinks too highly of themselves, they too can be highly aggressive. They suffer from a sense of entitlement and they have high expectations of the world. When their expectations are not met, they may become angry and aggressive. Their sense of entitlement is often so high that they will feel totally justified in their anger and have no remorse, because they feel they have done nothing wrong.

Being Addicted to Anger

Anything that gives us a 'high' can, in time, become addictive. Anger gives us a feeling that we are in the right, that we are powerful and strong as we fight for our position. But anger can be dangerous, and keeping ourselves in that state is moving us closer and closer to violence. Moreover, due to the fact that we feel we have every right to be angry, we become blind to the consequences to others. Over time, the 'high' of the angry state can become embedded in our brains just like any addiction (see Chapter 20).

CASE STUDY: JOE AND HIS ANGER

Joe was a father who attended one of our parenting classes on the recommendation of his social worker, as he had real difficulty in managing his anger. Joe grew up in a tough environment where the strongest person always won out. He had been in prison for assault, and was now out on parole and attempting to re-establish a relationship with his wife and children. His anger was getting him in trouble yet again, and he was in danger of having his children removed from him if he didn't learn to parent in a less aggressive way. He realised that he was, in fact, addicted to being angry and to getting his own way. This really shocked him, as he had never considered that a person could be addicted to anger. He decided that he wasn't going to let anger rob him of his relationship and

---

family, and he vowed to take control of it. We taught him 7/11 breathing (see Chapter 15) to help him calm himself. When the series of classes finished and we were reflecting on what had been learned, he told us that the most useful thing for him had been 7/11 breathing. He believed that it had kept him out of prison and had saved his marriage and his family.

It is clear that anger can easily escalate into violence. When anger takes hold and gets completely out of control, the angry person may experience extreme shame afterwards. Even worse, the target of our anger may have been quite traumatised by our attack.

Trauma

Sometimes, an old traumatic event (perhaps dating back many years) may be the driving force behind outbursts of excessive anger. Getting the help of an experienced professional can really help to neutralise the emotional arousal triggered by the original trauma.

CASE STUDY: JANE'S RAGE

Jane developed a huge rage problem when she was about fifteen years old, causing her dreadful problems at home and with her friends. Up until this time she had been a pleasant young girl, eager and willing to help out and popular at school. But now she would fly into a rage at the slightly provocation. She was very upset by this as she really didn't feel she could control it and didn't want to behave in this way. She was not able to identify the situations that were triggering the rage.

When we spoke about her life and what had occurred prior to developing this rage, she disclosed how she had been humiliated in school by a teacher for her writing and how some of the other girls had joined in and continued to jeer and slag her over the following months. She had felt huge shame at the time, and had become isolated from her classmates as every time she met these other girls the original shame was triggered again, whether they teased her or not. Anger and rage had become her way of defending herself whenever she felt she might be subjected to any kind of teasing or slagging. Unfortunately, one of her older brothers and her father were particularly fond of teasing as a form of playful banter. This resulted in her throwing tantrums at home and also snapping at her friends when she was at school.

When Jane understood that her brain was trying to keep her safe and protect her whenever it predicted that she might be teased, she saw the problem in a different light. We reframed her anger as an overly protective bodyguard and a 'rewind' (see 'Rewind Technique' in Chapter 18) of the humiliation she experienced as a result of the comments from the teacher and her classmates was very effective in helping her manage her anger and calm herself.

MANAGING ANGER – SOME USEFUL TIPS

Learning some skills to help you manage your anger can make a huge difference to your own health and to your relationships. Having anger management skills yourself means that you will be better equipped to help your teenager. Both you and your teenager might find the tips below useful. First, it may come as a surprise to you to learn that it can take as little as twelve minutes to get back to your normal self after a period of extreme anger. However, in order to achieve this, you have to commit to practising various different ways of calming yourself down.

- Learn to relax and calm yourself (see Chapter 15 for some good tips on relaxation).
- Manage your own stress levels whenever you can.
- Ensure that your emotional needs are met in balance.
- Monitor your self-talk and imagination, to ensure that you are not rehashing past grievances and using your imagination destructively.
- Take time out and get some exercise: this can help reduce the levels of the stress hormone cortisol as well as help you to calm down.
- Separate yourself from your anger. In other words, do not identify yourself as an angry person. *It* is not *you*, and you can learn to manage it.
- Become aware of unhelpful pattern-matches (see below) and detach them if you can. If you find this difficult, get a professional therapist to help you.

- Take time to learn to listen, negotiate and develop more effective communication methods and strategies (see Chapter 9).
- Remember that you are a role model for your children, and think about the consequences of what you may be teaching your children about the use of anger.
- Learn to handle criticism in effective ways, irrespective of whether such criticism is valid or not. Some useful tips on how to do this are outlined below.
- Learn to say 'No' clearly to unreasonable demands.
- Protect yourself from violence by removing yourself if you feel that a situation is dangerous or a person is getting very angry.

A Simple but Effective Breathing Exercise

7/11 breathing is also extremely useful in situations where you feel angry and know that you need to calm yourself down, or at the very least control your anger before you say something you will regret later. The 7/11 breathing technique (explained in Chapter 15) will help calm you and restore your equilibrium. The beauty of 7/11 breathing is that you can do it anywhere and no one will know that you are doing it. You can do it on a bus, in a car, at a meeting or wherever you are becoming overwrought.

Uncoupling Unhelpful Pattern-Matching

Often difficulties in managing anger result from unhelpful pattern-matching. This is a very common occurrence and results from how our brain operates naturally. Sometimes we get extremely angry at some small occurrence as it unconsciously reminds us of other times this has happened. Consequently, the emotion we feel is totally out of proportion to the event. An example of this is Maria, who was bullied in her primary school by another girl who constantly interrupted her. She didn't feel able to stand up to the other girl at the time. Now, as an eighteen-year-old, she becomes completely enraged if anyone interrupts her. She finds this very difficult to control and is very upset by it. If you find yourself in a similar situation, getting the help of a good professional therapist who uses the rewind technique (see Chapter 18) will really assist you in doing this.

Challenging Anger

If you are someone who has a lot of angry, resentful thoughts, a useful way to take back control of these thoughts is to challenge them. Try to become aware of your angry, negative thoughts because if you indulge them or encourage them they will continue and develop into an angry, resentful monologue in your head, which will lead to more and more stress hormones being released, further fuelling your anger.

Steer yourself away from angry thoughts. Try saying 'Stop' or 'Don't go there!' to yourself and tell yourself that you will not let an angry thought take hold of you no matter how justified it seems. Challenge the content of the angry thought by examining it rationally. Try to stand back and observe it objectively. Often, we accept a negative thought without questioning it. Try not to be too hard on either yourself or others, as the more you challenge these thoughts the less you will resort to them. Reframing them as outlined below can really help you to see them in a kinder light.

Reframing

'Reframing' is the term used to describe a technique that allows us to see a problem through a different frame, making it easier to cope with. For example, a negative thought such as 'My son is so controlling. He has to do things his own way, and won't do what I want!' can be reframed as 'My son is growing into his own man and is learning for himself what works for him. If I trust him, perhaps he will learn from experience, just like I did.' Or 'My daughter is so disorganised, she forgets everything and I have to remember everything for her!' could be reframed as 'Maybe she hasn't learned the skills of planning yet and could do with some help in developing them.'

A negative thought such as 'My dad hates me, he's always on my case' could be reframed as 'My dad really doesn't like the way I'm behaving right now; maybe if I changed how I spoke to him we could get along better. He wasn't like this when I was younger.'

Dealing with Angry People

Remember when dealing with an angry teenager that they are highly stressed and emotional and that their accusations may not make sense.

153

Try to look behind their anger to see what emotional need is not being met. Focusing on the need that is not being met can help both of you. When you are accused of something in an angry, accusatory way, try to remember that the other person is emotionally aroused and may find it difficult to articulate their feelings in a considered fashion. (This may be particularly so if that person is a teenager.)

There are three different ways to deal with an angry person, whether or not their anger is justified:

1. *Agree:* The idea here is to agree with some part of what they are saying. This will confuse them as it is not what they expect. Saying something like 'Yes you are right. That was probably a bit insensitive' or 'You may well be right. I may have been mistaken' gives the other person the benefit of the doubt.

2. *Admit:* Here, the idea is similar. Admit that you did something that could be considered negative. This helps the other person calm down and allows the conversation to move to a more productive stage. Saying something like 'Yes, I did make a mistake' or 'Yes, I have kept you waiting' is the best way to deal with your mistakes. It is also not expected. You *can* take responsibility for your mistakes without feeling guilty about it. It increases the other person's respect for you. This is particularly important with teenagers and children, as it models behaviour for them. Hopefully, as a result, they too will admit to their mistakes, and acknowledge that we are all human and screw up sometimes.

3. *Disclose how you feel:* Simply stating how you feel can be a powerful way of dealing with someone who is trying to manipulate you. For example: 'I realise you are upset that I can't lend you money, but I get so anxious when I am very short of cash myself, I find I don't sleep. So, I decided not to lend money to *anyone* any more. I'm so sorry I can't help.' This technique is also useful when you need to have a difficult conversation with someone else, including with one of your children. An example here might be: 'I feel hurt when you don't listen to me' or 'I get upset when you shout at me or the younger ones. Perhaps you can find another way to get rid of your frustration?'

If your teenager or someone else has a genuine complaint and is angry, their complaint does need to be heard. Repeat back what they have said and let them know that you have heard them. Tell them that you regret what has happened, and apologise to them. We all make mistakes and it is important to acknowledge responsibility when appropriate and look for a solution that will satisfy everyone involved.

If you are dealing with someone you know to be violent, it is important not to provoke them into further violence. Try to remain calm and understand how they are feeling; acknowledge that they are upset, frustrated and angry. It is important not to patronise them or fight back, as this may exacerbate an already volatile situation. Take any physical precautions you need to take, and remember that sometimes the wisest thing is to remain silent in such a potentially dangerous situation. It is important to stay physically safe; therefore, a good strategy is to ensure that the violent person is not positioned between you and the door. Be aware of the quickest exit route. In time, you can look for a longer-term solution to the situation.

17

Teenagers and Bullying

Bullying is not a harmless rite of passage; it can have serious effects on both the target of the bullying and the bully themselves. It is associated with an increased risk of mental health problems in later life in the bullies and their targets. Bullying affects many young people and, unfortunately, it is not always taken as seriously as it should be by those involved, or by the adults responsible for their care. Where a child is being bullied, how the child's parents, guardians and teachers handle the problem (i.e. whether or not they take it seriously and can successfully resolve the situation) can determine whether the bullying incident causes problems later in life.

What Causes Bullying?

As you will recall from earlier chapters, humans have innate emotional needs for security, attention, competence, control, friendship, community, status, privacy, meaning and purpose. These innate needs leave all of us at risk of succumbing to aggressive behaviour in order to meet these needs. Teenagers are particularly susceptible as they can become very focused on success and status (academically or in sports, hobbies or interests). Displaying their own unique skills and abilities to their peers and others becomes important to them. There are many aspects that contribute to an episode of bullying – the culture or environment, the perpetrator(s), the target and the bystanders – and each aspect may have to be addressed if the behaviour is to stop.

WHAT CONSTITUTES BULLYING BEHAVIOUR?

Bullying is defined as unwanted negative behaviour – verbal, psychological or physical – conducted by an individual or group against another person (or persons) and which is repeated over time. Bullying behaviour manifests differently, depending on gender and circumstances, but is comprised mainly of four different types:

- *Physical:* hitting, scratching, punching
- *Verbal:* teasing, making threats, name-calling
- *Emotional or relational:* excluding or isolating, scapegoating
- *Cyberbullying:* via social media, texting, email, chat rooms, video recordings and photographs

In a typical bullying situation, the perpetrator initially focuses on some fact about their target – some perceived difference such as their appearance, religion, behaviour, family background, illness, academic ability or popularity. Once they know the target will be affected by their taunts or behaviour, they continue to escalate their aggressiveness, to include lies, threats, scapegoating, isolation and possibly even physical assaults.

BULLYING CULTURE

A bullying culture can develop anywhere people come together and interact in groups, be that at home, school, sports clubs, workplaces, book clubs, professional associations, neighbourhoods or religious groups. The attitude of the adults or leaders of the group will either encourage or dissuade bullying. Teachers, parents, sports coaches and others who themselves use bullying tactics can act as role models for young people, so it is important to look into your own heart and ask yourself if you are unconsciously engaging in bullying behaviour that could be emulated by the teenagers around you.

Bullying by someone who is perceived as an authority figure can give licence to others to engage in similar behaviour. When it does, it needs to be addressed; otherwise, the bullying will be repeated even after that particular episode has been dealt with. Unfortunately, when the leader of a group (e.g. a school principal, sports coach or parent) is a bully themselves, outside intervention may be needed in order to address the behaviour that is creating the culture.

THE PERPETRATOR

The perpetrator's behaviour stems from a strong need for control, security, competence and/or status. It is most often used as a way to assert dominance in order to meet the perpetrator's needs. It is sometimes thought that engaging in bullying derives from a lack of social skills, but this is not the case. In order to successfully carry out a strategy of covert bullying or relational aggression (harm to someone's relationships or social status), a teenager needs highly developed social skills. The teenager who uses aggression in this way is often very socially aware, and not necessarily socially lacking. They need to be very sensitive and socially intelligent so that they know strategically when to strike and be successful. Such behaviour tends to develop in early adolescence, when teenagers are beginning to discover themselves. It also tends to coincide with a time when they are focused on what is cool and popular, and how to be attractive to other people.

While it is obviously hurtful to exclude people from a group or spread malicious rumours about them, these tactics work well in meeting the perpetrator's need for control. However, when such behaviour is rewarded by their peer group, the effect on the teenager can be very powerful. The rewarding response of respect, awe and increased status from their peers will mean that they will be compulsively drawn to continue the aggressive behaviour, and this will undermine any contrary messages communicated by teachers or parents. The rewards of respect, awe and status are partly why other teenagers do not reject this behaviour. The teenager with high status and recognition will seem more independent and adult-like, which is highly valued among their peers.

Research suggests that those who bully fall into one of two categories. The first category is those with low self-esteem: those who are not part of a group and who have failed to 'fit in' in some way. They are often poor academic performers and have a negative attitude in general to life. Their needs for attention, competence, status and belonging to a group are not being met, and they attempt to meet these needs in unhealthy ways through domination. Their motivation is often envy and jealousy of those they perceive as more competent or popular, and they resent those getting the attention and status they themselves desperately need.

Envy and jealousy are normal emotions, and when used positively they can act as signposts – pointing us towards what we need or want. They can act as motivators to help us achieve our own goals. When used negatively, they become motivators to dominate and be vindictive, thereby causing hurt to the target of the envy and jealousy. The aggression may also arise from the fact that the bully him/herself is or was bullied at home or elsewhere and they are just repeating behaviour that has been inflicted on them. It is an attempt to boost their self-esteem or to conceal a sense of shame or anxiety. The aggressive behaviour helps them feel empowered.

Somewhat surprisingly, the second category is individuals who have high self-esteem (or, perhaps more accurately, *too high* self-esteem). These individuals have high status and are often very popular. Their high status goes to their heads; they are often arrogant and narcissistic, and they succeed in maintaining their status through fear. Teenagers who fall into this second category tend to be very positive about life; they also enjoy school, as they are getting their needs met, albeit in very unhealthy ways.

Neither of these groups of individuals are getting their needs met *in balance*. Their aggressive behaviour results in a feeling of power and that can be very rewarding. Once this reward pattern has been established in a teenager's brain, it can act as a powerful motivator to repeat the aggressive behaviour, as it temporarily increases their self-esteem. In brain chemistry terms, what takes place is similar to the reward system (see Chapter 20). If the behaviour continues, it can result in creating a very destructive way of relating to other people in the future. Therefore, it is important to address this behavioural issue early on (before it becomes entrenched), so that the teenager can learn to meet their needs in healthier ways.

Remember, bullying is destructive for both the perpetrator and the target, as both experience extreme stress due to their needs not being met; furthermore, it creates unhelpful pattern-matches in the brain for both. If you are concerned that your child may resort to bullying behaviour, addressing this issue is discussed below.

THE TARGET

There are many misconceptions about the reasons why certain people become a target of bullying. Common ones are because the target is weak in some way, has social problems or that they somehow brought it upon themselves. Another misconception is that if the target were stronger or less sensitive they wouldn't be bullied. The fact is that *anyone* can be the target of bullying – anyone ranging from introverted or anxious youngsters who may not have many friends to popular, confident, competent teenagers.

There are many reasons why individuals are targeted. Anything that makes you stand out, positive or negative, can be the notional 'reason' for bullying, such as physical appearance, race, religion, wealth or lack thereof, family background, or academic, artistic or sporting ability. For example, a teenager could be bullied for being 'stupid' and 'slow' or for being a 'swot' and 'teacher's pet'. Unfortunately, many bullied teenagers often accept responsibility for their situation because they feel they are in some way to blame for their plight. It is important to emphasise to the teenager who has been targeted that they are in no way to blame; any indication to the contrary would merely compound the hurt they are already suffering.

Effects on Those Who Have Been Targeted

In cases where the target of the bullying sees it as 'their own fault' (that they brought it upon themselves in some way), they will ruminate over what they could have done to avoid it and what they could do now. They will be on 'hyper alert', acutely aware of the threat of future aggressive incidents. The combination of stress and rumination that ensues may lead to loneliness, depression, anxiety and, in extreme cases, suicide.

If, on the other hand, it is dealt with effectively, and the target is supported and goes on to stand up to the bully, they can grow from the experience and emerge with increased self-confidence that will serve them well in the future.

BYSTANDERS AND SILENCE

Bullying sometimes takes place in the presence of a group of bystanders (which can include 'friends' on social media). Bystanders often remain silent observers; their silence may be due to fear that they will become the next target. Alternatively, their silence can be an expression of vicarious satisfaction of their own jealousy, envy, fear or dislike of the individual who is being bullied.

The significance of the part played by bystanders in bullying is often underestimated or overlooked but bystanders play an important role. The bystanders' silence creates an illusion of support for the bully, which increases the fear of speaking out or objecting to the treatment of the target by other members of the group. Fundamentally, such behaviour further isolates the target and gives licence to the perpetrator. The bystanders may be unwilling or unable to recognise the effect of their silence on both the perpetrator and the target. If, however, they do speak up and take the side of the target, the illusion of support will be broken and the aggression will more than likely stop, as the perpetrator will have less support.

Unfortunately, the truth is that we can all be the perpetrator sometimes; equally, we may be targets or bystanders at different times in our lives. Stamping out acceptance of bullying requires us to own up to and confront our own behaviour, and to have the courage to take a stand.

DIFFERENCES BETWEEN BOYS AND GIRLS IN THEIR BULLYING BEHAVIOURS

Boys' and girls' bullying behaviours manifests in different ways. Boys' behaviour is usually a physical or verbal assault, whereas girls tend to use more verbal tactics, such as mockery, name-calling, giving the silent treatment, isolation, exclusion, or disclosing secrets or embarrassing moments. This is sometimes referred to as 'relational bullying' as it primarily affects the target's relationships with others.

LOCATIONS AND TYPES

School

While bullying can take place anywhere, school-related bullying is one of the most common types. It can occur travelling to or from school, or in the school buildings or grounds. Such behaviour may be indirectly supported by teachers and school staff either consciously or unconsciously by 'turning a blind eye' or through subtle or covert exclusion or humiliation. This apparent support for the perpetrator can be even more hurtful than the bullying itself, and will have a much greater effect on the target as a consequence.

Home

As a parent, your own need for control or security may be expressed through controlling your children to an excessive level. Unfortunately, this conveys an unhealthy message to your children of how to meet their needs and it gives them a false idea of what is acceptable behaviour towards others. The opposite can also be true. Difficulty in confronting and taking charge of your teenagers can result in giving them too much control, and can result in the teenagers acting like bullies with their parents.

CASE STUDY: JENNIFER

One of the worst cases of a child bullying a parent that I have come across was where the widowed mother, Jennifer, moved out of the family home into a flat nearby because her needs were causing problems for her young adult son, her only child. She worked hard: earning money, preparing nice food, ironing his clothes, cleaning up after him. However, once her requests for him to clean up himself became too much for him, he demanded that she move elsewhere if his lifestyle was causing her a problem. So, she found a flat and moved out. As the weeks and months went by, she continued cooking his food and cleaning the house (as he demanded she should do) while he was at college.

When he was a young child, she had lavished attention on him. She had given him too much control from an early age, especially after his father's death. As you can imagine, by the time she sought professional help, she was at her wits' end. Unfortunately, her parenting style was partly responsible for creating this scenario. As a result of two or three therapy sessions, she changed her approach to how she handled him. This took a lot of strength and resilience on her part, but she made the necessary changes and was able to return to her own home within a few weeks.

Consider the example you are setting and remember that your children are hugely influenced by your behaviour, even though it may not seem so.

Sibling Rivalry

Sibling rivalry is very common (and perfectly normal), but if it gets out of hand it can lead to one child bullying another. If you are worried that this may be the case in your family, consider the following questions: is one child in the family making life miserable for another? Is one child constantly the target of another child's aggression? Such aggression may not be physical; it could verbal or relational, which can be just as harmful.

Parents can sometimes unwittingly play a role in supporting this behaviour by not intervening in aggressive fights between siblings. A parent's failure to intervene can be unconscious through having a favoured or 'weaker' child or by making allowances if a particular child has a physical disability or emotional difficulty. The failure to intervene can give an unhealthy message to the favoured or 'weaker' child that they can get away with hurting others, and it can give the other child an equally unhealthy message that they have to accept such treatment.

Cyberbullying

Research has shown that the more removed we are from the experience of another's pain and hurt, the more likely we are to be cruel; this can explain why cyberbullying can be one of the most insidious forms of bullying, one where the worst cruelty can occur. Cyberbullying has become much more prevalent with increased internet use, and with the widespread use of social media. Misuse of cyberspace can be a very effective tool, as it allows for easy disclosure of embarrassing videos or photographs. Websites and forums that allow users to remain anonymous enable others to engage in posting cruel taunts and messages without repercussions.

Social media can also be used positively as it can give more power to a group of 'virtual' bystanders. These bystanders can isolate and shun the perpetrator and, just in the same way that distance can give people licence to be cruel, it can also make them braver and provide a platform for them to speak their minds and protest.

'Gay-Bashing'

'Gay-bashing' is the term used to describe verbal or physical abuse of members of the lesbian, gay, bisexual or transsexual (LGBT) community, or anyone who is perceived to be a member of that community. Gay-bashing has been receiving quite a lot of media attention recently. Members of the LGBT community now speak more openly about their experiences, which is highlighting the issue and, hopefully, will help to reduce it or stamp it out.

How to Recognise if Your Child Is Being Bullied

Some of the signs/symptoms that might suggest that your child is being bullied include:

- Physical signs – such as unexplained bruises, scratches, cuts or damage to their school uniform/gear
- Having few friends, or not being invited to parties
- Pains, headaches and stomach aches that have no apparent explanation
- Deteriorating homework and schoolwork
- Coming home hungry – this may indicate that their lunch is being taken from them
- Asking for or stealing money – the perpetrator may be demanding money
- Changes in behaviour – becoming withdrawn, anxious, irritable, unhappy or distressed
- Changes in appetite
- Talking about death or suicide, or attempting suicide
- Refusing to divulge what is bothering them

There may be many reasons for such changes in behaviour, so it is important not to jump to conclusions. But, equally, it is important to take note of the changes and spend time with your teenager, teasing out what lies behind the changes.

Boys are sometimes more reluctant to want to talk about what is going on, or reveal that they are being bullied; they may perceive it as a sign of weakness. Or, their reluctance to divulge information may be because they have been threatened not to talk. So, if you suspect that your teenager is being bullied, take your time when communicating with them and give them plenty of opportunity to open up (see Chapter 9).

WHAT TO DO IF YOU SUSPECT YOUR CHILD IS A PERPETRATOR OF BULLYING

If you suspect that your teenager is either a perpetrator or a target, it is best to deal with it quickly. If it is ignored, it will only escalate and communicate unhealthy messages to all involved. The perpetrator will feel that their actions are being rewarded, and the teenage brain is wired to seek reward. If an unhealthy behaviour delivers reward, it can end up being very destructive. An increase in status or control through bullying will cause the release of dopamine and endorphins. This 'reward' will create an unhealthy template that aggression is a legitimate way to getting their needs met. Unfortunately, the more of this behaviour they engage in, the more entrenched the behaviour may become, as it can appear to meet the perpetrator's needs, albeit in a very unhealthy way. The brain is also designed to repeat behaviours that are rewarding. For the sake of all involved, the sooner aggressive behaviour is confronted the better.

To tackle this, you need to understand that what they are doing is trying to get their needs met, and not blame or judge them. You will need to help them understand *what* need they are seeking to meet and then find a healthier way of fulfilling that need. You could use the Emotional Needs Audit (see page 144) to help identify the need in question. Then you can explain that the way they are doing so is inflicting harm on another person and not helping themselves in the long run. They may find this conversation very uncomfortable, but by not judging them and reframing their behaviour as a means of getting their needs met, they will be more open to understanding how they are hurting their target and experiencing the pain of hurting another person. By helping them choose healthier ways of behaving, it may be effective in stopping them repeating it. But your intervention really needs to be carried out with compassion and kindness, as they would not be resorting to such unhealthy behaviour if their needs were being met in more healthy ways. They too need support and help.

WHAT TO DO IF YOU SUSPECT YOUR CHILD IS A TARGET OF BULLYING

If you suspect your child is the target of bullying, you need to take it seriously. How you respond will depend very much on what is appropriate in the circumstances. Sometimes, your child will want to deal with it by themselves and this may be appropriate in certain circumstances, particularly in the case of a bullying episode that has just started or where they enjoy plenty of support from their friends and family. Teenagers are usually keen to handle things themselves. Knowing that they have the support of an adult can give them enough self-belief and confidence to take the necessary action on their own.

Initially, it might be appropriate to ignore the bullying. For example, in the case of verbal bullying, ignoring it is a simple but effective way to deal with the problem. Usually, the protagonist is simply trying to elicit a response, and if they don't get one they may desist (because their strategy is not working). If your teenager walks away from the verbal bullying encounter with confidence, this can work really well. It is important, however, that they are aware of the effect of their body language: the wrong kind of body language, whereby the teenager's body projects a sense of submission, can give the game away and betray signs of fear. Acting 'as if' they are not afraid can be a great way to coach a teenager to appear confident and not give away any signs of fear or distress.

In situations where your son or daughter is being teased, encourage them to stay calm and collected. Their calmness may deflect attempts by the bully to continue with the teasing. Another good tactic is to 'laugh off' the teasing. Laughing it off is not what the bully expects, and so this reaction can confuse them. Remind your teenager of their ability to choose where to focus their attention. You can remind them (jokingly) of their ability to ignore *you* when they need to. Ask them (jokingly) how they do that, and suggest to them they can use this same ability to ignore the bully. Anything that confuses the perpetrator can work well. This includes the use of humour or being very nice to them

– reactions that will throw them because, again, neither humour nor 'niceness' are reactions that a perpetrator will usually expect.

Remind your teenager that they are more mature than the perpetrator(s). They can be the 'bigger person' in this situation, and not succumb to the other's tactics. They can walk away and feel proud of themselves for doing so. Get them to practise walking with an air of confidence or speaking in a confident manner. Confidence can be a great defence against verbal bullying, so ask them to imagine they are an actor in a play or a film, and that even though they may not *feel confident* right now, *acting confident* will help them to feel confident in a future conflict situation. Give them a mantra such as: 'Fake it till you make it.'

You could also get them to rehearse (in their imagination) feeling tall and confident around the bully. Alternatively, pick an example of someone you know they admire and ask them to imagine how that person would deal with the situation. Then, ask them to imagine themselves being this admired person, doing what they would do. Get them to rehearse how that person would respond and this will help to further develop their confidence.

Remind them of all their positive traits and abilities, of things they have achieved and are proud of. Recalling this list will help boost their confidence at a time when someone is trying to undermine them. If possible, get them to hang out more with a group and spend less time on their own. By surrounding themselves with other people, they will be creating fewer opportunities for anyone to pick on them. In these ways, a teenager can communicate the message that they are neither intimidated nor daunted by the bullying behaviour.

If the bullying is more serious than verbal taunts, and your teenager cannot handle this on their own, it is time to contact the relevant authorities wherever the bullying is taking place. Write down all the details of what has been or is happening. Talk to those in charge in a calm manner and bring the written details with you to the meeting. If you are armed with details of specifics, it will enable you to be more objective and be taken more seriously.

The relevant authorities will need to investigate the allegations and this may take some time. Remember, it is important for them to know what is happening on their turf. Moreover, there may be other individuals apart from your teenager who are also being bullied, and therefore the overall problem may turn out to be much bigger than you realise. If you hear from your teenager about another youngster who is being bullied, it is important that you encourage your teenager to give them support. Having your teenager as a friend or ally could give them enough confidence to report or confront the bullying themselves.

A FINAL WORD ABOUT CYBERBULLYING

Where cyberbullying is taking place, it is important to encourage your teenager not to respond to texts or emails, even though they may be anxious to do so. If they do not engage, the perpetrator will get bored and stop. Let your teenager know that if they respond to the messages, and try to explain or justify themselves, they will be showing the bully that they are upset – which is what the bully wants to achieve.

If the bullying is taking place on a social media site, block the perpetrator(s) and use the 'report' link on the site to make a complaint. Encourage your teenager to be careful of privacy settings, and control who has access to their profile and details. Suggest that they avoid sites that provide anonymity, as this can give licence to bullies to post abusive and hurtful comments. As the cyber world changes so fast, it is really advisable to stay abreast of the latest social media and get some knowledge of how they work. This will give you enough knowledge to be aware of other possible avenues that could be used to intimidate your teenager.

If the bullying is by text or phone calls, remember it is also possible to block these callers. Encourage your teenager to take a note of times and dates of specific communications, and keep a note of messages as evidence. This will give your teenager a sense of empowerment. But also suggest to them that they do not continue to read over the messages, as this will only serve to upset them all over again and start them ruminating. In addition to this, use the suggestions above to help your child to develop their self-confidence and sense of security.

18

Teenagers and Anxiety

While it may seem obvious, it is worth stating that *fear* is at the root of all anxiety. Anxiety is closely related to stress: indeed, some experts would argue that the two terms are interchangeable. Anxiety is a natural response to a perceived danger: it is a survival tool that acts to warn us of a possible threat and, without it, we could be at serious risk of harm. Teenagers are more vulnerable to anxiety due to the fact that levels of the stress hormone cortisol are generally higher in teenagers than in adults.

As we know from earlier chapters, anxiety (or anger) is what is experienced when the stress response is switched on in the brain. The switch is activated when our pattern-matching mechanism perceives something that it categorises as dangerous. Once the mechanism is turned on we freeze, and our brain focuses on taking in as much information as possible before deciding how to respond. In fact, we can sometimes get stuck in this freeze state for long periods of time, unable to respond until the threat has passed. We then respond by fighting or running away (the 'fight or flight' response), or we forget ourselves and focus on others and look for support (the 'tend or befriend' response).

All of these responses are innate and instinctive. The same stress response mechanism is at work in humans, and those of us who have good imaginations are more prone to anxiety taking over. As children and teenagers have great imaginations they are especially vulnerable because they may not have yet developed the ability to manage their imagination. When anxiety takes hold for a long period of time, it has an adverse effect on teenagers' sleep, appetite, friendships and social activities.

WHAT HAPPENS WHEN ANXIETY TAKES OVER?

If you understand what is happening when you experience anxiety, it will help you get a sense of control over it and reduce the debilitating effect of fear. Anxiety affects your body, your emotions and your mind in many ways.

Body

Once the stress response is triggered in your body, the hormones cortisol and adrenaline are pumped into your bloodstream to ensure you are primed and ready for action. Your muscles are injected with glucose (to provide energy), your breathing rate increases as you take in more oxygen (to fuel action), your heart begins to beat faster (to ensure extra blood arrives quickly to the appropriate parts of your body) and your emotional brain takes over so that you respond quickly and appropriately. But if you don't take action all these hormones will remain in your body, causing the symptoms you feel when we get anxious. The most common symptoms are a thumping heart; a sweaty, clammy feeling in your hands, feet or body; butterflies in your stomach; and a feeling of dread. Sometimes, your legs may shake or twitch as a result of the concentration of glucose in your muscles. At other times you may feel as if you have no control over your bowels or your bladder; it is not uncommon for adults and children alike to wet themselves in response to an extreme state of fear.

As your breathing changes, you may feel as if you are gasping for air or even choking. This is due to excessive breathing – an automatic reaction to ensure that your body has all the oxygen it needs. But, paradoxically, too much oxygen can also create the sensation that you are gasping for air.

If you don't understand what is actually going on in your body, these symptoms can seem very frightening, and will only serve to add yet another layer of anxiety to your already anxious state, and may indeed make it worse. Understanding why these symptoms are occurring can mark the first step in taking back control.

Emotions

Once you become extremely anxious, previous experiences of frightening physical sensations, such as feeling dizzy or choking, or embarrassing situations where you fainted or panicked, can immediately come to mind (through pattern-matching). This can further increase the fear you are already experiencing, ensuring that you get a double whammy – a combination of the current fear, plus the fear of repeating past experiences where you found it difficult to manage your anxiety.

Thoughts

When you are in an extremely anxious state, you will pattern-match to previous frightening experiences. This then generates fearful expectations in your mind, and so your thoughts become overwhelmingly dominated by fear. The thoughts generated from a fearful expectation will be catastrophic or exaggerated as your mind jumps to conclusions. Combine these fearful thoughts with fearful bodily sensations and you can end up creating fearful, terrifying expectations of the future.

LOOSENING THE GRIP OF ANXIETY

If these three aspects (body, emotions and thoughts) happen together, they can create an overwhelming, unrealistic fear. This may manifest as phobias, panic attacks, obsessive-compulsive behaviours or post-traumatic stress reactions, all of which can have a detrimental effect. Extreme anxiety can take its toll in other ways too, causing lack of sleep, nightmares and withdrawal from life. It is very distressing to either experience the tight grip of anxiety, or to witness it in someone you love and feel unable to help.

In reality, anxiety is not so powerful. Understanding the mechanism of anxiety and how it works – and knowing how to reduce it – will give you back your confidence and enable you to take control of the anxiety, so that you are back in charge of your life and not dictated to by stress hormones.

CASE STUDY: ANN'S ANXIETY AND FEAR OF VOMITING

Ann had been anxious all her teenage years; when she came for treatment, she was almost twenty years old. She was suffering from severe anxiety and had been prescribed antidepressants as well as anti-anxiety medication, and felt she couldn't manage her day without them.

She reported that her anxiety started with a fear of flying, when she was about twelve, on a flight with her parents; after the plane experienced some turbulence, she vomited. From this point on, she developed a fear of vomiting in certain situations. Throughout her teenage years, this fear grew and became a more generalised anxiety, manifesting particularly when she was performing, such as when she had to make a presentation, was being interviewed, or anytime she felt she was being judged.

Initially, this was treated as a vomiting phobia (emetophobia) with a 'rewind' (see 'Rewind Technique' on page 179). She experienced much improvement after treating the fear she had suffered on that first flight and subsequent flights. She was happy with the outcome.

I didn't see Ann again for about a year. When she returned, she said that her anxiety was back and causing her huge problems again. She had difficulty sleeping, found it hard to cope during the day and was losing weight. She had developed anxiety about eating and particularly about feeling full, as she felt this increased the probability that she would vomit. She was on antidepressants and anti-anxiety medication yet again. We spent one or two sessions developing strategies and techniques to help her manage her anxiety, as well as investigating other experiences in her early childhood that may have preceded the initial vomiting experience on the flight.

Ann was a high achiever and had always been very successful in both her academic and sporting careers. She was used to being praised and acknowledged by her parents and teachers, who were all very proud of her. Her anxiety was very difficult for her, as it was stopping her achieving certain things she had set out to do, and she felt hugely frustrated and hopeless that she would ever overcome it.

As we progressed and tried to identify the pattern that had triggered this latest bout of anxiety, she began to understand that her brain and her body were responding unconsciously. With this realisation, her self-blame and admonishment reduced. As this happened, and as she developed the skills to manage her anxiety, she became more curious about what exactly was triggering her anxiety. Along with the anxiety that she had been experiencing, she realised she also felt huge shame about her condition. This is very common: people often feel that any emotional difficulty is a failing or a weakness, and they will go to great lengths to cover it up. We explored other occasions when she felt shame, and she remembered other times she felt shame that were not associated with vomiting.

At this point Ann's eyes lit up as she realised that what she was really terrified of was feeling shame, and she consistently avoided anything that might elicit such a feeling. She was delighted with this 'lightbulb moment' as the revelation made complete sense to her. The common factor in all her fearful episodes had been shame, and fear of experiencing shame as a result of other people's negative perception of her.

The realisation that she was terrified of feeling shame, along with her understanding of pattern-matching and the emotional arousal that followed, made logical sense of her anxiety and gave her a sense of control and mastery over it. She also understood how all the hormonal changes she was going through at the time would have increased her self-consciousness and would have made her vomiting episodes all the more difficult for her. This new-found knowledge allowed her to feel more compassionate towards herself.

To really strengthen and support this knowledge and understanding, we did a 'rewind' of all the shameful experiences in her past, and she reported that she felt hugely empowered afterwards. Finally, after all these years, she felt she could understand and explain her reactions. Best of all, she now had the tools to help her stay calm in social situations.

TECHNIQUES THAT HELP REDUCE ANXIETY AND STRESS

Anxiety lies to you and convinces you that you cannot manage your stress levels and calm yourself. But it is possible to manage it, and the following techniques will really help you reduce anxiety. Remember that anxiety is an emotion, albeit a very powerful one, but it is still only an emotion. You are being emotionally hijacked. Your emotional brain has been taken over, and as a result you are not thinking clearly.

Your emotional brain is primitive and not very intelligent. Sometimes it helps to think of it as a frightened child or family pet in need of reassurance. So, putting time and effort into learning to calm it so that you can access your own intelligence will really stand to you in the long run. Develop the ability to relax and reduce your stress levels – this may take practice, but is a vital skill for anyone prone to anxiety. There are many techniques that can help you to calm yourself, and some will work better for you than others. Many of these are outlined in Chapter 15, such as 7/11 breathing, progressive muscle relaxation, guided visualisation and reframing.

Investigate and experiment with the ways that work best for you and then incorporate them into your daily life. Take a positive approach that you *can* manage your stress and anxiety and reduce the feeling that it has power over you. This will also help you take back control.

The AWARE Technique

The AWARE technique (originally developed by Aaron Beck) can be a really useful way to help you manage your anxiety. The name is an acronym:

A: Accept that you are getting anxious. Don't fight it. That will only make it worse.
W: Watch the anxiety, try to step outside yourself and observe it without judging it as good or bad. Scaling the severity of the anxiety from 1 to 10 may also help.
A: Act normally. Do not run away from the situation: it will only bring short-term relief. Staying where you are gives your brain the message that you are okay and that this crisis will pass in a few moments. You could use 7/11 breathing (see Chapter 15) to help you relax.

R: Repeat the above three steps. Continue to accept that you are anxious, watch, be aware of it and act normally, rather than tensing up and becoming more frightened.

E: Expect the best. Try not to allow yourself to catastrophise and think of all the negative things that might happen; that will only make things worse. What you fear may never happen. Be confident that the anxiety will pass if you allow it to.

It is not possible or even desirable to get rid of all anxiety, but getting rid of panic most certainly is. Remember that you are *separate* from your anxiety; it is not an intrinsic part of you. It is something that either comes over you or creeps up on you without warning. But it is *not you*. You are not an 'anxious person'. If you label yourself this way, you will identify yourself with the anxiety and this will make it more difficult to manage. Instead, recall all the times when you were calm and relaxed. Identify with this aspect of yourself and remember that the anxiety can pass quickly.

WAYS TO MANAGE PANIC

A panic attack is a sudden overwhelming feeling of acute and disabling anxiety. Your heart pounds, you can't breathe and you may even feel like you're dying or going crazy. It can be very frightening. Panic attacks can be a one-time occurrence or a repeated experience. It can help to reframe a panic attack as an alarm (like a burglar or smoke alarm) that is being set off for some reason. Most times when an alarm has been activated it is due to something trivial, like burnt toast.

Remember that, from a physical point of view, your body is being flooded with stress hormones. When this happens, the automatic physical response is to begin to take short, fast, shallow breaths, i.e. to hyperventilate, in order to inhale more air. We do this automatically – to ensure we have sufficient oxygen available to deal with the threat.

When you don't use that available oxygen, it is breathed out again, but it takes carbon dioxide with it, thereby reducing the levels of carbon dioxide in the blood. The fast, shallow breathing throws the oxygen/carbon dioxide balance in your bloodstream out of kilter, and this causes many of the uncomfortable symptoms associated with anxiety, such as palpitations or dizziness.

Sometimes panic attacks occur as a result of a trauma and if this is the case the rewind technique (outlined on page 179) can make a huge difference to the experience. Panic attacks themselves can be traumatic and rewinding past experiences of panic attacks can also make a significant difference.

Here are some ways that you can help yourself – or someone else – deal with a panic attack:

- As you now know, if you are experiencing a panic attack, your body is being swamped with stress hormones. A good way to rid the body of some of these unwanted hormones is to take some aerobic exercise. Go for a brisk walk or a run. Alternatively, if you are confined indoors for whatever reason, run up and down the stairs or walk fast from one room to another. This will burn off the excess oxygen and help you to calm down.

- Focus on your breathing. Remember that fast, shallow breathing is only useful to you if you are about to take immediate physical action. When you don't take such action, this type of breathing only results in uncomfortable symptoms, which leads to more distress. An old remedy, which is very effective, is to breathe in and out of a paper bag. Exhaling carbon dioxide into the paper bag and inhaling that air again helps restore the loss of carbon dioxide in your bloodstream that has occurred as a result of the panic attack. Getting the oxygen/carbon dioxide mix back into balance will reduce some of the uncomfortable physical symptoms. Bear in mind that you need to stop breathing in and out of the paper bag once you begin to feel calm. Otherwise, continuing could result in causing your blood to have too much carbon dioxide, which could lead to dizziness, nausea, vomiting and other unpleasant symptoms.

- Another effective way to control a panicky feeling is to breathe in and hold your breath for a count of ten, and then breathe out slowly. This interrupts the automatic response and allows you to take charge of it.

- If you are in a public place and do not wish to draw attention to yourself, a very discreet way to reduce the panic symptoms is a form of breathing known as the 7/11 breathing technique (see Chapter 15). 7/11 is a very simple breathing technique that can really help calm your emotional brain, even when you are in the throes of a panic attack. If you practise it regularly, you will experience its efficacy and it will become second nature to you, giving you confidence that you can remain calm even in the most threatening situations.

Stress, anxiety and panic are all manifestations of fear. Remember that anxiety management can be learned. The various methods outlined in Chapter 15 will help you develop these skills. Find the one that works best for you. We all need to develop the ability to relax mentally or physically and take time out of life. It will help you think more clearly and make wise decisions.

TRAUMA

Anxiety in teenagers and adults sometimes develops after a traumatic event such as a physical, verbal or sexual assault, bullying incident, sudden loss of money, redundancy, car accident, heart attack or some other shocking incident. Frequently, the connection between the traumatic incident and the onset of anxiety goes unnoticed, and the person may be quite unconscious of what is precipitating the anxious feelings that are overwhelming them.

Trauma occurs when someone experiences an extremely dangerous situation, perhaps even a life-threatening event. The trauma is more likely to be accentuated if the person is also undergoing a lot of stress at the time or is very young.

Trauma can be caused by many factors. A case in point is the huge number of people who were traumatised by watching the 9/11 attacks in New York in 2001. Images of planes crashing into buildings were played over and over again for weeks on end on television, and these had a negative psychological effect on some people who had no connection with the victims. It resulted in them losing their sense of security, and they began to feel more anxious and threatened in their own lives. Similarly, hearing accounts of other people's traumatic experiences, stories of the horrors of war, or imagining the suffering of someone who has died and to whom you were close, has also been known to cause trauma – a phenomenon known as 'vicarious trauma'.

The majority of people process traumatic events by calming down and bringing perspective to bear on the incident in question. They realise that the event is highly unlikely to happen again, or they see that they were in the wrong place at the wrong time, that it was just sheer bad luck. In this way, they process the event within a few weeks and resume normal life. Other individuals can have great difficulty dealing with a trauma due to circumstances that make the trauma more difficult to process. A young child or a teenager may not have developed the cognitive abilities to enable them to do this, or others may have a very creative imagination, which can make them more vulnerable to trauma.

A person who is already under a lot of stress at the time of the trauma may find it more difficult to recover and the number of previous traumas they have suffered can also have a bearing. Stress is cumulative, so the traumatic event may be 'the straw that breaks the camel's back', so to speak. For some people, talking about the trauma can make it worse, as they end up reliving it each time they talk about it, thus causing it to become more deeply embedded in their memory.

Some of the after-effects of a traumatic event include symptoms such as recurrent thoughts or images of the event; nightmares of being helpless; flashbacks where they feel they are reliving the event; or severe anxiety when something triggers the event: for example, smells, sounds or images that bring back memories of what happened. This may lead some people to avoid anything associated with the event, e.g. certain forms of transport (trams, trains, buses, aeroplanes), certain people or conversations about the trauma. They often feel detached from other people, and frequently lose interest in activities they used to enjoy. They may find that their sleep is disturbed, find it difficult to feel close to others, have little hope for the future, have difficulty in concentrating, have outbursts of anger, be easily startled and may generally feel very anxious for no apparent reason.

After perhaps months or even weeks, they can slowly drift into depression. Or, they may turn to alcohol or drugs to help them deal with the distress of the anxiety and the triggers that are all around them.

So, What Happens When Someone Is Traumatised?

When you perceive a situation as very threatening, the amygdala in your brain becomes highly stimulated and triggers the release of vast amounts of cortisol and adrenaline into your blood stream. The brain's hippocampus works closely with the amygdala. Its job is to help process an event by creating a context for the situation. For example, it identifies that the snake you are looking at is no threat to you because it is on television, or that the sound of the screeching tyres is far away, and the car is headed in the opposite direction, so you are safe to cross the road. It is the hippocampus that helps you put a frightening situation into context.

However, when your cortisol levels are very high, it can reduce communication with the hippocampus and the neocortex. This leaves the primitive amygdala trying to process the event. The amygdala is only capable of very crude pattern-matching, so it codes everything associated with the event as 'terrifying', meaning that everything that is remotely associated with the event must be avoided – even if it is totally harmless.

Normally, within a few weeks of a traumatic event, the person's stress levels reduce, and the communication lines open up once again. The event can be put in context by the hippocampus and the memory of the event can be stored away in the long-term memory. The person can think about it calmly and logically. Unfortunately, this does not happen in all cases. When it does not happen, the memory is still stored as a crude pattern-match in the amygdala, and so an upsetting event that happened in school when you were twelve can be triggered again at fifty if the memory hasn't been processed properly.

Speaking in public is a common example of this. If someone was shamed or ridiculed as a pupil in school for their lack of reading ability or fluency, this memory can be triggered again any time that person is asked to speak in public, resulting in feeling great fear and panic. While the person may acknowledge that the panic is unreasonable, they are unable to control the high anxiety that the prospect of speaking in public creates in them. In order to treat the trauma, the person's amygdala needs to be calm enough to process the original event in the correct context, and then recode the event differently for the future. A safe, quick way to do this is the 'rewind technique'.

Rewind Technique

Briefly, the rewind technique works as follows. The traumatic event needs to be activated once more, but without allowing the amygdala to get terrified again. The person is asked to imagine that the event has been recorded on a DVD. They are then asked to visualise themselves playing the DVD on a television set (so that they are distanced from the event); this allows them to recall the event while remaining calm and prevents the arousal levels from getting too high. They are then asked to go backwards through the event, and, as this is an unnatural thing to do, it requires that they engage their neocortex. The trauma is then re-experienced in a calm way, allowing them to process the memory naturally.

The trauma can then be put in the past, where it belongs, and we get the message: 'It happened in the past, and we are safe now.' Granted, the memory of the event will always be there – and will remain unpleasant – but, following rewind, the memory will no longer generate fear and panic in the same way.

The amygdala of someone who has been traumatised has been imprinted with the pattern of the trauma. This imprint contains all the information surrounding the event: smells, sounds, colours, people and location. Whenever there is a match or a part-match to that imprinted pattern, the amygdala fires off the alarm reaction and an extreme stress response is activated. And because this all happens at an unconscious level, the person is only aware of the high emotion 'E' of APET: overwhelming fear (see Chapter 4).

It is because the amygdala only looks for *something like* the event that people experience flashbacks and other severe alarm reactions. *Anything* that has a similarity to *something* in the original traumatic event will cause this reaction. That is why the reactions can sometimes seem so illogical and mysterious to the sufferer.

CASE STUDY: ALISON'S PANIC

An interesting example of this was Alison, a twenty-year-old woman who had been suffering from anxiety, which was becoming progressively worse and had reached the point of preventing her going out and leading a normal life. When she presented for treatment it was obvious that she was very distressed. She arrived with her boyfriend, John, who sat with her and held her hand throughout the session. There seemed to be no specific fear that was triggering her anxiety, and she had reached the point of being afraid of fear itself. She had been a healthy, calm teenager, and this fearful state had only started in the previous two years. When asked if anything had happened two years earlier, she said her boyfriend's best friend, Tom, had died by suicide. This event had been very traumatic for her, but she believed it had nothing to do with her anxiety, and said she didn't think about it any more.

However, when she spoke about what happened, it was clear that the suicide still distressed her. She and Tom had been very close, and it was a very shocking death. His family was distraught and the funeral was particularly distressing. His family had gone to great lengths to ensure that it was a beautiful ceremony: the church was filled with his favourite flowers, Casa Blanca lilies.

It seemed appropriate to rewind the event, and she readily agreed if it would help her anxiety. A week after the rewind, she reported feeling much calmer. She was sleeping better and able to concentrate more; she was back to her old self, able to enjoy life again. She now realised it was the smell of lilies that was triggering her fear. Anytime she went to the supermarket or to someone's house where there were scented lilies she would become fearful because it triggered the distress of the funeral, and she had been utterly unaware of this association.

John then asked for a rewind, as he had been unable to work since his friend Tom's death. After witnessing Alison's rewind session and recovery, he was very clear about what was triggering his own symptoms. His friend had hanged himself with a rope. As John was an electrician and worked on wiring newly built houses, he realised from Alison's experience that his trauma was triggered every time he saw loops of electrical wire hanging from a ceiling. Looking at such a scene caused him to feel nauseous and dizzy and, as a result, he had been unable to work. After the rewind, he too was able to return to work and get on with his life.

Trauma and Teenagers

Because some children or teenagers have particularly good imaginations, they can be easily traumatised by seemingly harmless events. They can terrify themselves with their own imaginations, or as a result of hearing stories of what happened in a war or some other horrific event. Television programmes, films, YouTube clips and even video games can all affect children far more deeply than adults, and sometimes what seems harmless to an adult can have a seriously detrimental effect on a younger person.

CASE STUDY: MELANIE'S STRANGE SYMPTOMS

A dramatic example involved an eleven-year-old girl, Melanie, who was suffering from very strange symptoms for about six weeks. Up until this point, she had been a bright, healthy, happy young girl who was doing well in school and was popular with her classmates. She began sleeping very badly, having nightmares and tossing and turning so much that she woke up exhausted every morning. This behaviour pattern progressed to wetting the bed, which she found particularly distressing. Finally, she began to lose all feeling in her arms and couldn't move them. Her parents naturally became very worried and took her to the family GP, and also to see a paediatric neurologist. She was hospitalised for tests but nothing abnormal showed up in the results. Her parents were at their wits' end as to how to help her when they brought her to me.

Initially, it wasn't at all clear what was causing the problem, but what was clear was that she was afraid to fall asleep because of the nightmares. The first session involved rewinding all her memories of the nightmares. This was an important first step, as it meant she could sleep better. After the first rewind session there was some improvement in her condition: she was sleeping better and she had regained some limited movement in her arms. So, in our second therapy session, I asked her, 'What was the scariest thing you have ever experienced?' She immediately replied that it was the afternoon she went to the cinema with her aunt. The film they saw was about the kidnapping of a girl who was being held for ransom, and the story of her parents' fight to get her back. In the film, the

---

girl was kept in a dark room by her kidnappers, her hands were tightly bound together, and no one spoke to her. She was given food and drink, but she couldn't move off her bed. This meant that she sometimes wet herself, as her kidnappers didn't respond to her calls for help. The story centred on the parents' search for her, and how they took matters into their own hands (as they do in movies). In the end, the girl was rescued and reunited with her parents. She was hailed as a heroine in her school and all turned out well.

When Melanie was asked why she found this movie so frightening, she said it was because her aunt told her it was a true story. This really frightened Melanie, but she never mentioned it and she did her best to forget about the movie, and put it at the back of her mind.

It seemed that Melanie had been so affected by the movie that she was experiencing the physical symptoms of the kidnapped girl. After completing a rewind of the movie, and the conversation with her aunt, Melanie's arms were no longer numb. That night – and each night thereafter – she did not wet her bed. She slept well, reverted quickly to her old self, and was back at school within a few days.

This understanding of what is happening in the brain when we are traumatised – and how to treat the trauma – can avoid the distressing symptoms that really disturb people's lives. The same process of pattern-matching underlies the problem of phobias. A phobia is also the result of a frightening experience that was imprinted at some point on the amygdala, and is now being reactivated. Phobias can be treated quickly by using the rewind technique.

Professional Help

If anxiety continues to cause difficulty, it may be necessary to seek professional help. It may be necessary to help the person process and neutralise an experience that is the root cause of the anxiety. This can be done with the rewind technique. The rewind is a safe, quick way to neutralise the fear that has prevented the traumatic event from being processed. As a result, the trauma then continues to affect everyday life with intrusive memories, nightmares and constant anxiety.

Human Givens therapists use the rewind technique to great effect to resolve all kinds of traumas, such as car accidents, personal attacks, severe sexual and physical abuse, bombings, bullying and many other terrifying events.

If you feel that a rewind is something that you may benefit from, remember it is a skilled procedure and should only be carried out by an experienced practitioner. You will find information on where to find practitioners in the Useful Resources section at the end of this book.

OTHER NOT-SO-USEFUL COPING MECHANISMS

Sometimes coping mechanisms may become a bigger problem than the anxiety itself. People – and teenagers in particular – often turn to alcohol, recreational drugs such as marijuana, or prescription drugs such as Xanax to relieve anxiety. This can give the false belief that a pill or a substance is necessary to control anxiety. The real truth is that these substances can have a negative effect on mood and motivation, and can become addictive if the person becomes dependent on them in order to stay calm.

Others turn to food: either they eat to give themselves comfort (which may lead to excessive weight gain), or they attempt to control their eating (which may lead to anorexia and bulimia). Some people get angry and blame others for their anxiety (which can ruin their relationships). Others go shopping and avoid paying bills (which can lead to mountains of debt). Sometimes they find that the anxiety can be relieved in the short term by repeated behaviours such as constantly checking if the door is shut or constantly washing their hands, or a preoccupation with violent, sexual or religious thoughts. While they may be aware that these thoughts and behaviours are irrational, they continue with them to relieve their feelings of anxiety and panic.

CASE STUDY: JOHN'S OBSESSIVE THOUGHTS

John was sixteen when he came to see me with his mother. He had been diagnosed with anorexia and obsessive compulsive disorder (OCD) three years previously. He was extremely anxious: he controlled his food and his eating, and had frightening thoughts about hurting others, particularly children. As a result, he avoided children whenever he could.

John was afraid that he had been contaminated by some kind of poison. He thought that he couldn't control himself and that he was a danger to others. He was afraid he would contaminate or harm them, even though consciously he didn't want to harm anyone. These thoughts resulted in him controlling his food intake, staying hyper-alert and avoiding vulnerable people as much as he could. Inevitably, this affected his health and his sleep, and he had become very hopeless. His dream was to become a doctor and now he felt that he couldn't pursue this.

There were a number of events in his past that had badly shocked John. He was unjustly accused of bullying. He was very concerned that his friends would believe his accuser rather than him. He kept repeating 'There is no smoke without fire', and he obsessed that he must have done something, even though he couldn't figure out what. He ruminated a lot about his reputation with his friends, some of whom had given him the cold shoulder. His fear developed to a point where he felt he couldn't control his behaviour; he worried that he would contaminate others and that he was the cause of all the difficulties in his family.

He had also been badly upset by a family row and by events in the news at the time – specifically, the disappearance of four-year-old Madeleine McCann in Portugal and reports of the extent of sexual abuse of children by religious orders. These news stories added to John's fear. He had no trust in himself; he believed his thoughts were controlling him and that he would act on these irrational thoughts to harm or contaminate others.

These events, especially the bullying accusation, had completely shocked him and created huge anxiety, but after I explained APET to John, how his stress levels were creating these fearful thoughts, and also how our brains respond to shock, he calmed down. The shock had badly affected his sleep, and he was unable to think straight and began to doubt himself. He was certainly not thinking clearly at the time.

After rewinding these events, I taught John 7/11 breathing and emphasised the difference between thoughts and behaviour.

I further explained that his dark thoughts were generated by the primitive, emotional brain, and that it is very common to have fear-driven thoughts that you would never act upon. Armed with this knowledge, he became considerably calmer.

When I saw John again, he was doing much better and his parents had seen a huge improvement both in his demeanour and in his eating. In addition, his anxiety was drastically reduced. He was still a bit anxious about his thoughts, but doing a visualisation of seeing himself training to be a doctor, and becoming competent and trusted, really helped him to relax about his thoughts, which over time receded.

John returned to me a few years later when he was in the process of completing his medical studies; he had become very anxious again. The problem had started when he was required to complete a work placement at a local hospital. It transpired that he had been a patient at that hospital when he was anorexic. Now, many years after his original time there as an in-patient, John was pattern-matching, and was experiencing similar emotions to when he there the first time. When he realised that his anxiety had been caused by pattern-matching he calmed down; this helped him take control of his anxiety and, once again, revert to his calm self.

FACE YOUR FEARS

Using the information in this chapter and practising the relaxation techniques described above will help you move into your 'observing self' – that part of you that helps you direct your attention away from your emotions and onto behaviour and activities that help you take control of your anxiety. The way to overcome your anxiety is to face it and learn to manage it. Remember, you do not have to do it alone. If you need to, find a good therapist to help you, and you will experience increased self-confidence as you take charge of your own anxiety and achieve more in your life.

19

TEENAGERS AND THE BLUES

At some point during the teenage years almost every young person will assume a look of disillusionment, glumness or boredom – most likely due to a combination of factors, not least the huge hormonal and physical changes in their bodies. They are trying to forge an identity for themselves while dealing with a confusing world, so it is not surprising that many young people become disillusioned with what they see going on around them.

However, the disillusionment and boredom of teenage years is not the same thing as real depression. Real depression is characterised by a debilitating lack of motivation and interest in normal activities that the teenager previously engaged in or enjoyed. As a parent, you need to take such a fundamental change in behaviour seriously and get professional help for your teenager.

As you will know from reading the various topics covered in earlier chapters, whenever someone's emotional needs are not met, irrespective of whether they are an adult or a teenager, they will begin to ruminate about how to resolve this. For example, take a teenage boy who hasn't got a girlfriend while many of his mates do. This boy will begin to think obsessively (often unconsciously) about how to go about getting a girl, and he will worry and ruminate about how to solve the problem and secure some female attention for himself. The same holds true for a teenage girl who is not part of a group. Being left out and considered 'not cool' will cause her to try to solve the problem, become part of a group, and meet her need for community and belonging.

Constant rumination generates a lot of emotional arousal, whether that be worry, anxiety, frustration or anger. Add self-blame or recrimination to this and the result will be increased worry and rumination, which generates even more emotional arousal and stress – a vicious circle. When anyone is feeling emotional they cannot think clearly. Indeed, when you are in this state, your 'emotional brain' can only think in black-and-white terms; it is not capable of the complex thinking of your logical, rational brain. So, irrespective of the nature of the original problem, the process of ruminating – and the resulting emotional arousal – causes your thinking to become polarised into 'all or nothing' or catastrophic scenarios. For the teenager, this may manifest as 'I'll never get a girlfriend', 'I'll never be part of the group' or 'No one can help me.' Or, if they are frustrated or angry it may manifest as 'I'll show them!' or 'I'll get them back!'

Once we become emotional, we activate the stress response – preparing us to take action. A person who is ruminating is doing nothing: they are stuck. This results in their levels of cortisol and adrenaline increasing dramatically. The presence of too much cortisol coursing through the bloodstream sends both your body and your mind into overdrive, affecting the neurochemicals in your brain. If you do not 'process' or complete the stress response by taking action or reconnecting in some way, i.e. doing what nature intended, the stress response remains incomplete and will need to be processed. It is while you are dreaming, i.e. experiencing REM sleep, that you finish processing the stress response.

Dreaming is the natural way of processing and discharging unexpressed emotions, so in itself it is a good thing. But too much dreaming has a major downside: the more time you spend in REM sleep, the less time you spend in the non-rapid eye movement (NREM) stage – enjoying the refreshing, restorative sleep that is essential if you are to feel motivated, enthusiastic and able to function properly the following day (see Chapter 12).

Anyone who is constantly ruminating will spend a disproportionate amount of time in REM sleep at night. REM sleep burns a lot of energy – the very energy that you need for motivation. The result of too much REM sleep and not enough NREM sleep means that when you wake the next day you will feel tired and lack motivation. You will almost certainly have experienced this yourself on occasion – waking up exhausted, feeling as if you haven't slept at all when, in fact, you have been asleep all night. It's not that you haven't had *enough* sleep; it's that you haven't had enough of the *right kind* of sleep – the refreshing, restorative sleep that you get when you are in the NREM stage.

Normally, when a stressful period in your life passes, or when you resolve a particular problem, this cycle of experiencing too much REM sleep stops and you return to your normal sleep pattern. However, if the increased REM sleep continues over a prolonged period, it can develop into a cycle, where lack of energy and enthusiasm results in creating new worries. So, on top of worrying about the original problem, you are now worrying about why you have no energy.

In the case of teenagers, if this unhealthy sleep cycle continues – and they have less and less energy available to engage with the world – they are likely to withdraw, increasing the amount of time they spend ruminating, which in turn causes them to become more and more depressed. A vicious cycle indeed.

HOW TO RECOGNISE DEPRESSION

Symptoms of depression may manifest in teenagers in different ways. For example, they may stop engaging with their friends, they may drop a sport they used to enjoy, or they may become withdrawn, which in turn causes them to ruminate. As they ruminate more, they become increasingly negative, unable to see solutions to their difficulties. When their emotional brain takes over, the 'all or nothing' perspective becomes predominant. Teenagers are notoriously moody, and it is often tricky to ascertain the difference between depression and ordinary teen moodiness.

Here are some symptoms to look out for. If any of them have been present for more than two weeks in your teenager, this may indicate that they are suffering from a depressive episode:

- A sad, irritable, cranky mood and a belief that life is meaningless
- Loss of interest in activities they used to enjoy
- Withdrawal from friends or family, or trouble in relationships
- Changes in appetite, either weight gain or weight loss
- Changes in sleep, either too much or too little, staying up very late, trouble getting up in the morning
- Changes in physical behaviour – either increased lethargy or agitation, pacing or excessive repeated behaviours

- Loss of energy, boredom and withdrawal from usual activities
- Being overly critical of themselves, exhibiting behavioural problems at school or at home, being overly sensitive to comments by others
- Changes in performance in school, or more frequent absences from school
- Frequent physical problems – pains, headaches, etc.
- Obsessing about death, giving belongings away, or making comments such as 'You'd be better off without me'

While many of these symptoms of depression are also common in normal teenage behaviour, being aware of them can help parents deal with the problem as quickly as possible. Left untreated, depression can have serious consequences, and therefore speedy intervention is important.

How to Help Lift Depression

If you suspect that your teenager is depressed, try to find out what changes in their life have preceded this low mood. Let them know that you are concerned, and encourage them to open up and share what is causing them distress.

- *Offer support and understanding:* Hold back from asking too many questions, no matter how anxious you feel. Teenagers don't like being crowded and, to them, being asked a lot of questions can feel like being subjected to an interrogation. Make it clear that you are ready and available to provide whatever support is necessary.
- *Encourage them to open up:* They may be reluctant to open up, they may feel ashamed or afraid of being misunderstood, or they may find it really hard to express what exactly they are feeling. If they are adamant that nothing is wrong and can offer no explanation for the changes in their behaviour, trust your own instincts and act accordingly.
- *Be gentle when talking to your teenager:* Try to put yourself in their shoes. As you know, the teenage years are difficult and confusing. Resist the urge to criticise or judge them when they do begin to open up. The most important thing is to just listen and avoid giving unsolicited advice. Try to acknowledge how they feel and how

difficult it must be for them – even if what they are saying seems irrational or silly to you. If you take their feelings seriously, they will feel that they are being listened to and understood.

Gender Differences

Remember that when it comes to opening up, there are some subtle differences between the genders. Teenage girls, for example, are often more willing to seek help, or to open up to a parent with their problems. If your teenager has more of a connection with one parent than the other, then that parent should take the lead in facilitating the 'opening up' conversation.

Often, sitting at the kitchen table over a mug of tea or coffee is all that will be required to initiate such a conversation with a teenage girl. Boys, on the other hand, can be more reticent when it comes to speaking about what's going on in their heads. So, one of the simplest things you can do is organise a car journey alone with them. Males (teenage and adult alike) seem to find conversation easier and less intimidating if they don't have to maintain direct eye contact with the person they are talking to.

If you don't have a car or you don't drive, then find some other activity that you or your teenager can share while you are chatting together. Perhaps initiate a conversation while you are engaged in some household task – cooking, painting, gardening – or while you are out walking the dog.

Remember that not all boys or girls respond alike. Experiment with different approaches when encouraging communication, and make a note of which approach works best with your child. Remember that the most important thing is to suspend judgement of your teenager's thoughts and actions, and resist the urge to give unsolicited advice; this can rapidly close down a conversation.

Other Dos and Don'ts

- *Encourage physical activity:* Encourage your teenager to be physically active. Exercise can make a big difference in helping to lift depression. Find ways to incorporate exercise into your teenager's daily routine. Even simple things such as taking the dog for a walk or cycling to the shops can be beneficial. If your teenager is reluctant to take exercise, it can help to explain the science of the stress response and how exercise can help process the cortisol and adrenaline generated by stress and will help them sleep better.

- *Encourage social activity:* Withdrawal from social involvement and depression often go hand in hand. Unfortunately, withdrawal and isolation only makes depression worse, so it's important to encourage your teenager to see their friends. Where practical, offer to drive them to meet their friends, or take them and their friends to an event, such as a concert or something else that they are interested in. Try to get your teenager to focus outwards, and encourage them to engage in activities they have dropped or are avoiding.

- *Learn about depression:* Learning more about depression can really give you confidence when dealing with a depressed teenager, but it is important to ensure that your sources are reliable. A full list of helpful resources is outlined at the end of this book. Perhaps explain how rumination causes sleep patterns to change, leading to excessive REM sleep and insufficient NREM sleep, and that this is why they are so tired in the morning, and lack energy and motivation throughout the rest of the day.

    It is important that whatever material your teenager is reading – either on the internet or in books, newspapers or other media – is not overly negative. What they need most at this time is hope that whatever they are currently experiencing will pass. There is always a danger that the black-and-white thinking of the emotional brain will succeed in convincing them that their current situation will never end, and that things will always be like this. Therefore, ensure that they get the message that depression can be treated and that there are lots of things they can do to help themselves.

- *Stay involved and interested in their treatment:* If your teenager is seeing a professional such as a counsellor, therapist or GP, stay involved in their treatment. Watch for changes in their condition, and contact the GP or other mental health professional if their depression seems to be getting worse.

- *Look for solutions to whatever has caused the depression:* Help them look for solutions to their problems. If they are being overly emotional, they will be unable to think clearly and may not have considered some of the more obvious solutions that are available.

Suggest that they complete an Emotional Needs Audit (see page 144). This will help them identify what needs are not being met in their life, and will point the way to possible solutions.

- *Deal with traumatic incidents:* Sometimes, a teenager gets depressed after a traumatic incident such as the sudden death of a loved one, a suicide, an accident, a relationship break-up, an unexpected failure (e.g. exam- or sports-related) or bullying. At times like these, a teenager may be unable to emotionally process what has happened and, as a result, they may worry and ruminate so much about these events that they eventually become depressed. In these situations, a good therapist will be able to help them deal with the traumatic event and get back to focusing on the future.

- *Watch out for suicidal thoughts:* Possibly the most distressing thing that could happen to any parent is that their child takes their own life. Left untreated, depression can end in suicide, as the depressed person sees no way out of their difficulties other than suicide. So, for a depressed teenager, avoiding alcohol is vitally important, as alcohol suppresses normal inhibitions and may inadvertently enable someone to choose the suicide route – something they might not have done if they were sober.

What is most important is to do whatever you can to help reduce their emotional arousal, which will help the teenager out of 'black-and-white' thinking. Emphasise the temporary nature of all experiences and do what you can to create hope. If you are seriously concerned about a teenager, get appropriate help for them in whatever way you can, either through their GP or other health professional.

Do not underestimate the traumatic effect that a friend's suicide or attempted suicide can have on a teenager, as they try to make sense of their friend's decision. It can really undermine their sense of security when someone they know appears to have made such a drastic choice out of the blue. The suicide of a friend or schoolmate can also have the effect of making such a choice seem attractive – particularly if the death or subsequent funeral received a lot of attention. The depressed teenager may only register the attention, the accolades and the tributes – and not the devastating consequences and finality of the suicide choice. So-called 'copycat' suicides are therefore a real danger for an already depressed teenager.

If you think your teenager may be suicidal, get professional help. Signs of suicidal thinking should never be ignored.

CASE STUDY: MAGGIE AND RUTH'S DEPRESSION

Sisters Maggie (eighteen) and Ruth (seventeen) separately sought appointments with me. They were both looking for help with dealing with their depression. As it happened, their difficulties stemmed from the same event in both cases.

Their father had bought a lot of property during the boom and, following the credit crunch that began in 2008 and the economic recession that followed, the family were under extreme financial pressure. Because their father had overextended himself financially, his restaurant business was now almost bankrupt; he was also in danger of losing the family home along with all the other properties he had acquired over the years. Due to the extreme pressure he was under, and in an attempt to find a solution to his predicament, he reckoned that his wife and family would be better off financially if he were no longer alive; on this basis, he made the decision to end his own life. Luckily, he was found in an unconscious state by Maggie, who called the emergency services, and he survived the suicide attempt.

Unsurprisingly, Maggie was badly shocked by finding her father in such a state, and began to suffer from anxiety and depression. She found it hard to fall asleep and was in a constant state of high alert, even though she wasn't aware of it at the time. Ruth, on the other hand, had a different reaction, and although she too was depressed, she had become very angry with her father, shutting him out of her life and maintaining her relationship with him only at a superficial level. Both girls had come to regard their father as uncaring and selfish, and believed he didn't care about them. They felt hurt and let down and, naturally, they were also on tenterhooks, afraid that he would make another suicide attempt.

When both girls learned about APET and how the emotional brain affects a person's thinking, they could easily understand that they were seeing things from their own viewpoints only. They began to look at things from their father's viewpoint, and understand

---

that prior to his suicide attempt he had been desperately seeking a solution to his dilemma. He had been ruminating constantly and had not been sleeping. He was completely emotionally hijacked; the decision to end his life seemed to him like a good one at that time. He was not thinking clearly, and when he regained consciousness in hospital he was horrified by what he had done. I explained to Maggie and Ruth that when we are emotionally hijacked we all become temporarily selfish (our brains become consumed and obsessed with finding a solution to our problem); this insight helped them regard their father's behaviour differently.

Since their sessions (which included a 'rewind' of their experiences of his suicide attempt) they have come out of their depression, have been able to manage their anxiety and anger, and, critically, have been able to re-establish a relationship with their father. They have come to see their father more realistically and they are also more aware of his (and their mother's) vulnerabilities. These insights have enabled the girls to grow and become more mature than their peers, taking on responsibility and playing a more active role in the family. They are now armed with relevant knowledge about the negative effects of undue pressure and stress, and the importance of sharing and getting support in times of difficulty. In fact, both girls and their mother are now actively involved in the family business, and it has brought all of them closer as a family.

MEDICATION

Some parents may feel pressurised into choosing antidepressant medication over talk therapies for their teenage son or daughter, due to the financial cost or the time investment required to attend therapy sessions. Bear in mind that unless your teenager is considered at high risk for suicide, talk therapy is often a more long-term solution, and has been shown to be more effective in the treatment of mild to moderate depression.

While antidepressants have a role to play in the treatment of clinical depression, and may be prescribed for severe cases, they come with side effects and various risks, including a number of safety concerns. It is important to note also that antidepressants were designed for and tested on *adults*, not teenagers. Therefore, their impact on the young, developing brain is not yet completely understood. Moreover, some researchers are concerned that the use of antidepressants may interfere with brain development. The brain develops rapidly in young adults, and exposure to antidepressants may have an impact on that development, particularly on the way in which the brain manages stress and the regulation of emotions.

Some antidepressants may increase the risk of aggression in some youngsters up to the age of 25. The risk is highest during the first two months of taking the medication. Consequently, if your teenager is on antidepressants, watch out for warning signs such as increased agitation, irritability, anger or unusual changes in behaviour. If you notice such changes, refer back to the doctor who prescribed the medication.

WHAT ABOUT THE REST OF THE FAMILY?

One of the effects of dealing with a depressed teenager is that you may find you are devoting a lot of energy to addressing their needs and their problems. This is understandable, but in doing so you may also be neglecting your own needs and the needs of the rest of your family. It's important therefore to keep in mind the following:

- *Take care of yourself:* You need to stay healthy and positive and not ignore your own needs. The stress of dealing with a problem teenager in the family can affect your emotional health, so it is important that you get the right amount of sleep and rest.
- *Reach out to others:* If you are feeling overwhelmed, seek the support of your family and friends, or a consultation with a professional therapist to help you cope with the frustration or helplessness caused by your situation. Getting the right kind of support can help you through this testing time.
- *Talk to the other family members:* Talk to your teenager's siblings, as they will be aware that something is amiss. If there is no discussion about the problem, their imagination may run riot and they may come to dramatic – and inaccurate – conclusions. Depression in one family member can have the knock-on effect of causing anxiety and stress in the other children, so make sure that you also give your other children time and attention.

- *Avoid blaming yourself:* It is easy to blame yourself or another family member, or to worry about what you might have done differently. Such recriminations will only serve to increase your own rumination. Depression is often caused by a number of factors coming together, a 'perfect storm', as it were. Therefore, attributing blame or engaging in rumination will not be helpful to you or to any member of your family.
- *Be patient:* Living with a depressed teenager can be both difficult and draining. At times, you may experience exhaustion, rejection, despair, aggravation or any number of other negative emotions. During this trying time, it is important to remember that your child is not being difficult on purpose. Do your best to be patient and understanding as coming out of depression may take time. Praise your teenager whenever they make good choices, and be prepared for the occasional setback. Most importantly, don't judge yourself or compare your family to others. As long as you're doing your best to get your teenager the necessary help, you're doing your job.
- *Seek professional help:* When choosing a therapist for your teenager, always seek their input. Teenagers are dependent on parents for making many of their health decisions, so listen to what they're telling you. If your child feels uncomfortable or is just not 'connecting' with a therapist, ask for a referral to another who may be better suited to their needs, or who is perhaps just a better personality fit for your teenager.

20

Teenagers – 'Getting Hooked'

Unsurprisingly, parents can become very fearful and distressed at the prospect of their teenager engaging in any potentially addiction-related behaviour. They fear that they will get 'hooked' and go on to destroy their lives. Learning what is going on when someone becomes addicted will bring some perspective and help you calm your fear and panic and deal with your teenager's problem activities and substance abuse in a more composed and effective way. So, how do people become addicted and why is it that teenagers are more vulnerable than adults?

The 'Reward System'

The 'reward system' outlined in Chapter 7 is the basis of addiction. The chemical reactions that underlie this system leave us all vulnerable to 'getting hooked'. As discussed before, it is important that our physical and emotional needs are met in a balanced way. When our physical needs or emotional needs are met, we experience a feeling of pleasure. We get rewarded for doing something that meets our needs, and this reward ensures that we continue to meet those needs. This feedback loop is the 'reward system' in the brain and it is directly related to how vulnerable to addiction all humans are.

If you have experienced pleasure in the past by engaging in a particular activity, your brain is chemically programmed or encoded to *anticipate* pleasure if you repeat that activity again. You have created a chemically encoded pattern; a positive expectation of pleasure in your brain. If you anticipate repeating the activity, your brain automatically activates the encoded pattern and has the 'expectation' of re-experiencing the pleasure. It is this expectation that motivates you to continue to seek to meet your needs through engaging in that particular activity.

So, referring back to APET in Chapter 4, the 'activating agent' of meeting your friends creates a positive pattern-match and a positive expectation of getting your needs met. This process is enhanced by the release of dopamine, which is often called the motivation hormone – it gets you to *do* something. When dopamine is released, you are motivated to repeat whatever was responsible for delivering that pleasurable feeling in the first place, in this case meeting up with your friends. All of us are programmed to repeat pleasurable experiences from the past. It is how we learn. We repeat pleasurable activities that help us meet our needs, and we refrain from activities that are unpleasant and do not meet our needs. We are positively conditioning ourselves to continue a behaviour that is good for us.

All human beings are also programmed to try out new things, so that they can learn and grow. One of our emotional needs is to become competent and achieve goals in our life. Learning and growing encourages us to be creative and adaptable. So, not only do we have an innate need to grow and learn by trying out new things and expressing our curiosity and creativity, we are also rewarded when we do so. For example, think back to a time when you tried out a new activity: perhaps you took up a hobby, or tried out a painting class, or embarked on swimming lessons. Recall the 'high' you felt afterwards. This 'high' is what motivates you to do it again. You now have an expectation that you will experience pleasure again. This expectation is the 'carrot' that is driving you forward.

But, unfortunately, you never experience the same level of pleasure the second and third time you repeat the same activity, because if you did you would probably never try anything new again, and therefore you would never develop. The 'pleasure dial' is turned down. As the level of pleasure you experience reduces, you develop a 'tolerance' for the activity – you no longer get that initial 'high'. This is nature's way of ensuring you continue to try other new things and stretch and grow. Our brains are programmed to seek out new experiences.

If, on the other hand, you cease engaging in an activity that is good for you, you begin to get an unpleasant feeling and an urge to take up that activity again. The unpleasant feeling helps you to continue repeating the new activity; this feeling is often referred to as 'withdrawal'. For example, think back to an occasion when you might have stopped some activity that gave you pleasure (swimming, for instance). The uneasy feeling of withdrawal is what motivates you to take up swimming once more; it is the 'stick' that keeps you repeating something that is good for you.

This reward–punishment, or carrot–stick aspect of our makeup, which has evolved to help us learn and grow, is the same mechanism that addiction hijacks when we get hooked into an addictive cycle. It can work both positively and negatively as follows.

Take, for example, the familiar cycle of deciding to try something new in order to improve your life – a phenomenon that tends to occur around New Year, when people vow to take more exercise and get healthy, or make some other major life change. You might join a gym. You feel great as a result of the endorphins produced from exercising, and you return home on Day One on a 'high', promising yourself that you will repeat the exercise routine the following day. While the memory of the 'high' of the endorphins and the dopamine motivates you to repeat the exercise, the pleasure you get on Days Two and Three is never as great as the pleasure you got on Day One. And so your motivation decreases, and you are now experiencing tolerance. If you succumb to the television and the couch after a number of days of regular exercise, you experience a 'low' of something missing, and you feel worse. This 'low' is the 'stick' of withdrawal – pushing you to repeat a behaviour that is good for you.

Therefore, the learning process is a cycle: the 'carrot' of the 'high' that results from achieving something is followed by tolerance as these 'highs' reduce. Then you experience the 'stick' of withdrawal if you stop that behaviour. These highs and lows are what motivate you to continue doing something that is good for you.

THE 'CARROT AND STICK' AND DRINK AND DRUGS

The same 'carrot and stick' process comes into play with regard to something negative, such as when you take a drug or a drink that is designed to deliver an artificially induced 'high'. Your brain records this as pleasurable, and you are motivated to repeat the process again.

You have now established a pattern in your brain that associates instant pleasure with that particular drug or drink.

Whenever your life is not working well, and your needs are not being met, you become vulnerable to repeating something that gave you pleasure; this is because your brain has been programmed to *expect* pleasure from that substance. As a result, you repeat the drug-taking or drink-taking activity and, once again, you experience a 'high' of completing the expectation of pleasure, but it is never as good as the first time.

But unfortunately the pattern you have created in your brain is not only formed from the effects of pleasure generated by the substance, it is also linked to the excitement of trying something new. Then add other aspects associated with the experience – such as feeling part of a group, feeling accepted, increased confidence and status – all of these positive experiences combine to create a heady cocktail of pleasure associated with that substance.

As if that wasn't enough, addiction plays another trick on you. When the memory of the pleasure is recalled, it is laced with dopamine and it is therefore inaccurate; it has become a distorted, dopamine-soaked memory. The memory and the extent of the pleasure is a lie, it is promising you a level that you never actually experienced. The dopamine has increased the pleasure memory and has given you a false promise. This phenomenon is known as 'euphoric recall'; it creates an expectation of something that never actually happened in the first place.

If you choose to repeat the experience, you will have an expectation that you will experience immense pleasure. When you do not, it drives you to take more of the substance in an effort to re-experience that original 'high'. Taking more of the substance creates tolerance, and it is why an addict needs more and more of the substance in order to get high.

If a person decides that an addictive substance is really causing a problem in their life, and they decide to reduce their intake, the withdrawal symptoms will begin and they will experience pain. If the pain of withdrawal is too strong, it will only succeed in driving the person back to taking the substance once more. At this point, they now need the substance in order to feel just okay, as opposed to needing a substance that gives them pleasure. They are now well and truly addicted.

When a person uses a drug for the first time, their brain goes into crisis mode, but then recovers quickly. Like the rest of the body, the brain always attempts to achieve a normal healthy state of functioning (homeostasis). While alcohol and psychoactive drugs throw the brain off temporarily, it will work hard to get things back to normal. (A hangover is an example of this hard work being done by your brain.) However, when a person uses alcohol or drugs frequently, their brain adapts to being flooded by chemicals and it then perceives this as 'normal functioning'. At this point the person has become drug-dependent, and more and more of the drug is required in order for them to function at all. Research shows that teenage substance abusers become tolerant to abuse faster than their adult counterparts.

Once a person stops using a drug, the pleasure they used to feel is replaced by pain. So, someone who smokes cannabis in order to feel relaxed will feel anxious once they stop, or someone who uses cocaine to feel alert will feel sleepy and lethargic once they stop; this is because the brain needs to learn to function again without the assistance of the drug.

The process described above shows how the 'risk and reward' centres in the brain (which help you learn and grow) can be 'hijacked' by the false promise of a quick fix. In contrast, while the natural reward system in the brain focuses you *outward* (and encourages your curiosity and creativity in a positive way), addiction focuses you *inward* (and leaves you reliant on a substance or an activity in a negative/destructive way).

The difference between the 'high' achieved from exercising or learning and that delivered by drugs or alcohol is that the exercise or learning requires effort, and nature rewards effort. With drugs or alcohol, no effort is required, and so the reward is false. You have been tricked into thinking you were getting the real thing – the 'high' of achievement – when all you actually got was the artificial eurphoria created by a chemical substance.

The Moral of the Story Is …

Whenever life is not working well, and your needs are not being met, you are vulnerable to resorting to whatever gave you a 'high' previously, so that you can escape from the unpleasant feeling you experience when your needs are not being met. The way out of this trap is to understand how the reward system works, how you are vulnerable to it working against you (i.e. developing an addiction), and how you need to focus on meeting your needs in a more positive way.

WHAT CAN WE BECOME ADDICTED TO?

In addition to the obvious candidates (alcohol and drugs), other activities such as eating, shopping, sex, exercising, playing video games and gambling (or any behaviour that has the ability to give you pleasure or change your mood) can become addictive. As far as your brain is concerned, the addictive behaviour is helping you get your needs met – albeit through an inappropriate pattern-match in your emotional brain.

The brain's reward system can be activated by anything that gives pleasure, whether that is a high mark in a class assignment, winning a race, having sex, eating an ice cream or taking cocaine. The resulting dopamine rush makes it more likely that you will repeat the behaviour. Of course, cocaine will activate the reward system more powerfully than perhaps ice cream or winning a race but, nonetheless, the same neurological process is being activated in both cases.

TEENAGERS AND ADDICTION

Why are teenagers more vulnerable to getting hooked? They are more vulnerable due to their developing brain. The changes occurring in the brain during this period create a stronger urge for risk-taking. A teenager is primed to take more risks, to learn for themselves and to create their own identities. Unlike the adult brain (which is generally more cautious), the teenager's brain propels them towards trying out new, exciting things.

Chapter 7 outlined the double effects of dopamine and oxytocin, and how these hormones play a huge part in making teenagers more vulnerable to any addictive substance and behaviour. Once you understand the 'risk and reward' process, it can help you steer yourself and your teenager away from the harmful, false promise of addictive substances and direct them towards the healthy 'high' of achievement. Getting a teenager 'hooked' on achievement is leading them towards a road of growth and development, as opposed to the deadly road of addiction and where that leads ultimately.

Key Differences between the Teenage Brain and the Adult Brain in Addiction

The teenage brain is more susceptible to addiction because it is *programmed to learn through taking risks.* This makes it more vulnerable to addiction than the brain of an adult, whose risk-taking will have become progressively more measured from their twenties onwards. The teenage brain is also highly responsive to reward, and it becomes less active in the absence of reward. This may go some way towards explaining the intense boredom experienced by many adolescents.

The positive aspect of such boredom is that it provides a healthy motivation for the teenager to learn and to leave the nest. The negative aspect is that it provides a strong motivation for them to seek risky roads to pleasure. Unfortunately, because teenagers are more motivated by reward rather than by punishment they are less likely to imagine all the terrible things that might happen as a result of taking risks. Not only are they less likely to take into account the possible consequences, they are more likely to try out new risky behaviours and repeat pleasurable ones.

Most teenagers who overindulge in some addictive habit will eventually grow out of it as they meet their emotional needs in more healthy ways through relationships, sport, study, work, family, etc. They will also be helped by the development of their frontal lobes so that they have more control over the primitive, emotional brain. But until they get to that stage, which will be sometime in their late teens or early twenties, young people are more susceptible to succumbing to some addictive habit; they just have a harder time delaying gratification.

The positive aspect of dealing with teenage addiction is that the greater plasticity of teenagers' brains means they have a greater capacity to learn and recover from a period of addiction. Generally speaking, if they are motivated, the prognosis for such teenagers is much more positive than the prognosis for an adult who is addicted.

SYMPTOMS OF POSSIBLE DRUG OR ALCOHOL ABUSE

If your teenager displays the following symptoms, it may indicate that they have a problem with drugs or alcohol:

- Seems more moody than usual
- Has become secretive and apathetic
- School performance has disimproved
- Has developed a lack of interest in school
- Has less interest in their appearance
- Appears to lack energy and motivation

How can you recognise when such symptoms are problematic, and distinguish them from the normal mood fluctuations of the teenage years? Changes in behaviour, such as those listed above, are symptoms of a problem of some kind. However, they could equally be caused by many other problems in your child's life, such as bullying, depression and anxiety.

So, what are the other signs of possible drug abuse? Specific behaviours associated with possible drug abuse include the following:

- Secretiveness
- Spending a lot of time on their own
- Reluctance to allow family members into their bedroom
- Stealing money
- Looking for money, with no credible explanation for why the money is needed
- Lying
- Making excuses
- Staying out late
- Increased aggression
- Mood swings
- Sleeping problems
- Changes in appetite
- Depression
- Paranoia
- Difficulty concentrating
- Poor memory
- Agitation
- Change in friends or peer group

Other worrying signs include finding paraphernalia among their possessions associated with drug use, such as matches, cigarette papers, pipes, pill bottles, syringes and needles.

THE EFFECTS OF ALCOHOL AND DRUGS ON THE TEENAGE BRAIN

Alcohol

One of the difficulties with alcohol is that its use is so pervasive, and that it is so often regarded as harmless. But, of course, it is not harmless. In terms of the amount of potential brain damage it can cause, alcohol is not that different from other chemicals such as cocaine, marijuana or ecstasy.

The statistics associated with alcohol abuse are staggering. In a survey carried out by UNICEF in 2011, almost 50 per cent of teenagers reported that they got drunk for the first time when they were under sixteen years of age. Fifteen per cent of teenagers reported that they were under fourteen years of age, and the vast majority (just short of 90 per cent) said their parents were aware of their drinking.

In the context of potential damage to the young person's brain (which does not fully mature until between the late teens and mid-twenties), these statistics are truly shocking. It means that a significant proportion of young people will have subjected themselves to almost ten years of alcohol abuse before their brains are fully developed. Damage inflicted at such a vulnerable period in their lives is likely to have more lasting and serious effects.

So What Damage Does Alcohol Do to Teenagers in Particular?

Alcohol impairs learning, decision-making, impulse control, balance, language skills and vision in both adults and teenagers. When consumed in high doses, it affects the ability to breathe and also one's awareness of breathing difficulties, which is highly dangerous.

It can be difficult to determine just how much alcohol a teenager has consumed because, unlike adults, teenagers are less likely to fall asleep or lose their balance. Crucially, alcohol impairs cognitive function (including learning and decision-making) much more powerfully in teenagers than in adults. The same applies to judgement – which is much more adversely affected in teenagers.

Withdrawal from alcohol is also associated with major problems; it causes some neurotransmitters in the brain to become hyperactive, and this can either damage or kill brain cells. Scientists believe that the prevalence of binge drinking or repeated drinking bouts accounts for the difficulties in learning, memory and problem-solving that are typical among regular teenage drinkers.

Repeated alcohol abuse in teenagers results in poorer performance in learning, memory, spatial awareness, attention and concentration. Alcohol also suppresses the development of new neurons in the hippocampus and, as a result, the hippocampus in a teenage alcohol abuser's brain is smaller than the hippocampus in a healthy teenage brain. Scientists believe that the blackouts that many teenagers experience following an excess of alcohol are linked to a lack of neuron development in the hippocampus. In addition, alcohol abuse also stunts the growth of the corpus callosum (the brain structure that connects the right and left hemispheres) and the amygdala. It also interferes with the maturation of the frontal lobes, which in turn affects the development of healthy decision-making.

Most people are not aware of these facts. If they were, attitudes to drinking might be less tolerant and parents might regard alcohol abuse as potentially much more dangerous to their teenagers' underdeveloped brains.

Marijuana and Cannabis

The UNICEF survey cited above also reported that marijuana or cannabis ('grass' or 'weed') was the most popular substance used by teenagers who admit to taking drugs, with more than two-thirds reporting that they first took the drug when they were aged sixteen or younger. Grass has been synonymous with rebellion and coolness for decades. The key difference, however, is that the grass that today's teenagers is smoking is much stronger than the variety that was available years ago. In the 1970s, for example, the psychoactive ingredient in marijuana, tetrahydrocannabinol (THC), had a strength of 1 to 2 per cent, whereas today it is approximately 10 per cent, i.e. at least five times stronger.

Because it is a lot more potent, it has a much stronger effect on the brain.

Cannabis has mild to moderate analgesic effects and its use results in a very relaxed state; changes in a person's sight, hearing and sense of smell; fatigue; and increased appetite for food and drink. In larger doses, cannabis can induce auditory and visual hallucinations and can cause acute anxiety and euphoria.

Long-term use of cannabis poses the risk of damaging a person's ability to focus their attention on complex tasks such as driving. It has been shown to have a much more damaging effect on the learning performance of adolescents than of adults. Scientists believe this negative effect on performance is due to the damage that cannabis causes to the hippocampus. So marijuana, like alcohol, has fundamentally different effects on adolescents and adults.

Making reference to proven scientific knowledge about the effects of cannabis can provide a good starting point for a rational discussion with your teenager. Indeed, the potential effects of cannabis on academic performance and on social and sporting success might have a particular resonance for your teenager. A fact-based discussion is likely to be more beneficial for both of you than engaging in an emotional argument.

CASE STUDY: MICHELLE'S DRUG PROBLEM

Michelle sought help in the wake of a very distressing psychotic episode, which followed shortly after she had taken a variety of drugs at a music festival. She had been through a very difficult year, although at the time it didn't seem so to her. There was no shortage of money in Michelle's family; as a result, once she finished school and started college she had the freedom and the financial wherewithal to party without limit, which she did.

Michelle is a sensitive, creative young woman who, unfortunately, had chosen a college course that didn't really suit her. Consequently, from early on in the year she found herself struggling with her lectures and course work. She didn't want to admit to her mistake; she wanted to appear confident and independent, and she found that 'dope' helped her forget her problems and cope with her new life.

A few months into the college year, she broke up with her boyfriend after she discovered he was cheating on her. Gradually, she began to miss lectures and fall behind in course assignments.

She became very popular with her college mates because she always had a supply of dope; soon, she began to grow it in her apartment. The attention and popularity she earned from her friends seemed to compensate somewhat for the break-up with her boyfriend and her lack of interest in her college course.

Sometime around Easter she eventually told her family that she wasn't happy with her choice of course. She dropped out of college, citing plans to start another course the following September. She was at a complete loose end for about four months and decided to make the most of it and attend as many music festivals as she could. Given that money was no object, she also began to experiment with other drugs. She got into ecstasy and acid, and had some very positive experiences of getting in touch with the 'deeper meaning of life'.

Amongst her former college friends, she became known for having both money and access to drugs. The students who sought her out tended to be those who were on a destructive path to serious drink and drug abuse. These college 'friends' persuaded her to attend a music festival in England, where they planned to join her. She travelled on her own (to prove her independence and also to feel grown up) but when she arrived at the festival her expectations of her new-found 'friends' were dashed when she realised that they were only interested in her money to be able to buy drugs. To dull the painful feelings about this realisation, and in order to feel part of the festival, she went on an alcohol and drug binge. Within a short time, she ended up having a psychotic episode, during which she had some bizarre, terrifying experiences.

Michelle realised that she was on a very destructive path and that she had had a lucky escape. Thankfully, she was so shaken by the experience that it served to create a very healthy fear of alcohol and drugs and their potential effects. She learned how vulnerable we all are to succumbing to a 'quick fix' when our lives are not working and how a number of elements had conspired to make life difficult for her.

Having too much money can have a really negative effect, particularly on a young person. It interferes with the healthy connection between effort and reward. Michelle was getting the reward of money without exerting any effort, and then she got a further 'reward' from drugs, once again without exerting any effort.

To her credit, Michelle gave up all alcohol and drugs. When she learned about her emotional needs during her therapy sessions, she set about meeting them in healthier ways. She got a job at a local coffee shop to earn her own money, which gave her a sense of achievement and control. She experienced the healthy 'high' of earning for herself; she also found that she was very popular with the staff and customers because she had a lovely, bubbly personality. She decided she would use the time while she was waiting for her new course to start in September by learning to cook. That way, she could feed herself and not live on takeaways, as she had tended to do during her first year in college. She distanced herself from her college 'friends' and instead took up again with her old pals from school, including a girl with whom she developed a strong friendship.

She now understands the importance of ensuring her emotional needs are met, and leads a very healthy life. She is enjoying her new college course, and is doing well academically. While she drinks socially, she has no interest in or urge to use drugs again.

Nicotine

As countless research studies have proven, smoking is highly addictive and can cause cancer. For various reasons already explained, adolescents' brains are more sensitive than adults' brains to the 'reward' and stimulation effects of drugs such as alcohol, marijuana and nicotine. Because teenagers experience more of the rewards and fewer of the negative effects of smoking, this can further increase their susceptibility to tobacco addiction.

OTHER ADDICTIONS

Anything that gives us pleasure can become addictive, and this includes technology and internet use. The internet is an amazing tool that has transformed our lives, but like any tool it can be misused. Internet and video games exploit the reward centres of the brain to keep the players excited and engaged. The speed and instantaneous rewards of these games make them highly addictive and limiting their use is important. Chat rooms and social media are also pleasurable in that they meet our need for friendship and connection, but not in a true way; humans need social interaction in the real 3D world, not the 2D world of screens.

Self-Harming Can Be Addictive Too

There are many reasons why a teenager – or indeed an adult – self-harms but, usually, it is because they are attempting to deal with some kind of extreme emotional distress. Initially, the urge to self-harm may serve as a way to relieve extreme emotional pain by causing physical pain, such as cutting oneself. (The 'relief' derives from natural painkillers, endorphins, which the brain releases when we are physically injured.) Self-harming behaviour can become addictive. The memory of the initial relief that followed the person's first self-harming episode is laced with dopamine (euphoric recall) and they have the expectation that they will experience that 'high' again, which they don't, and so their self-harming behaviour becomes more and more entrenched.

MANAGING ADDICTIONS

The main way to protect your teenager from becoming addicted is to ensure that, as far as possible, their emotional needs are met in healthy, satisfying ways. Seek out and find ways in which your teenager can experience the natural high of learning and achievement in whatever area they are interested in, be that sports, drama, art or gardening, for example. Such activities create a real, natural high that is both sustainable and healthy.

If you are dealing with a current addiction (either your own or your teenager's), there are a number of stages to overcoming it. Once you or your teenager have come to the decision to make changes and deal with a substance or activity, you will have moved through a number of stages already. You will have accepted that what you are doing is not working, contemplated the required changes, become determined to change and are now ready for action. But research has shown that it is the next phase that can be the most challenging – the maintenance stage. To assist you in being successful, there are a number of essential steps to help you move through the maintenance phase.

Overcoming an Addiction

1. *Eliminate positive expectations:* If you are helping your teenager to overcome an addiction, explaining the 'false promise' of positive expectations may go a long way towards helping them to see the light. Other approaches worth considering might include arranging for them to have a conversation with older relatives or friends who have dealt with addiction, giving your teenager a book about someone whose life was ruined by addiction, or watching a film on a similar topic. The most important thing is, as far as possible, to change the positive associations with the substance or activity to negative associations and create positive associations with being free of the dependence on the substance or activity. Then, the 'carrot' will have lost its appeal, and the addictive substance or activity will be less likely to generate the 'euphoric recall'. You may need professional help to assist you in doing this.

2. *Revamp your/their lifestyle:* Consider whether either your current lifestyle or your teenager's lifestyle may be feeding the addiction. For example, is your/their social contact limited to a circle of people who are also involved in addictive behaviour? If this is the case, finding a new social group would be very important. Eric, a long-term alcoholic, moved to a town 150 kilometres away from his home in order to break the connections with his drinking buddies when he decided to give up alcohol. He created a new identity for himself in this town – one where his new friends never associated him with alcohol. This really helped him create a new life. While this is the extreme, choosing new friends, a new hobby or sport, or a change in college or course, can help your teenager meet their needs in a healthier way.

3. *Anticipate high-risk situations:* High-risk situations are times, places, people and things that will remind your teenager of the pleasure they *perceived* the substance was giving them when they first began to abuse it. If the addictive behaviour involves smoking or alcohol, then parties, sports events or celebrations of any kind, where they are bound to encounter people who are either smoking or drinking, fall into the category of high-risk situations. Put a plan in place to help them through this time successfully, by having strategies to fall back on should they feel they are going to succumb to addictive

urges. Such strategies might include phoning someone, choosing to leave a venue or choosing to replace the substance with something less harmful. Working on such strategies in conjunction with your teenager will increase the likelihood that any plan your teenager devises will be a success. In short, they are more likely to stick to a particular plan if they are the one who devised it in the first place.

Finally, remember there is expert help out there for you or your teenager. Look for a good professional to help you navigate high-risk situations and beat the addiction forever. See the Useful Resources section on where to get good professional help.

CONCLUSION

While the teenage years are tricky, and sometimes feel like a roller-coaster for everyone involved (including the teenagers themselves), it is good to remember that most teenagers develop into well-adjusted, balanced adults. Obviously, some teenagers have fewer resources and also have more challenges to face than other teenagers, and will therefore need more support in navigating their teenage years.

Should you find that you or your teenager needs additional assistance in addressing a specific problem, seek out professional advice. It can make all the difference between struggling and overcoming a particularly difficult period. When seeking professional advice, it is good to know that some psychological or psychotherapeutic approaches work better for teenagers and, certainly, long-term psychotherapy is not the best option for this age group.

Seek out a Human Givens or some other brief solutions-focused therapist who is experienced in dealing with teenagers and understands the particular challenges they undergo. Ideally, the therapist should have some knowledge about the teenage brain (both male and female) and should also be knowledgeable about hormones and their effects. Take note of your teenager's experience with the therapist, and ensure that they feel relaxed and at ease with this person. Your teenager's relationship with the therapist is very important. If they are not connecting with the therapist, see if you can find one who suits them better. (See the checklist in the appendix for advice on how to choose the right therapist for your needs.)

While teenagers can be challenging, and can try your patience to lengths you might not have believed possible, they are also confused, emotional, anxious and vulnerable. The more compassion you can muster for them, the more they will respond. In general, people want and need to be understood, and teenagers, more than others, are in dire need of understanding, as they themselves are greatly perplexed by some of the changes they are going through, and they have only a few years' experience to draw on to help themselves muddle through.

Thankfully, the teenage years come to an end, and, as any parent who has seen their teenagers emerge into their twenties will attest, these young people often surprise and astound you with the level of common sense and wisdom they have amassed during these turbulent years.

Today's teenagers are the adults of the future, and the more we understand and support them through their turbulent years, the more we will create a compassionate, caring and equal society for us all to thrive in. The more you can manage your own emotions, ensure that your own needs are met, and stay calm through the turmoil, the smoother will be the journey for all concerned.

Take good care of yourself, and of your teens. Having reached the end of this book and digested all this information and knowledge, you now have many more resources at your disposal to make a huge difference in their lives. Because even though it may not seem so, they actually do pay attention to what you say and do!

Appendix

Effective Counselling and Psychotherapy Checklist

It is a good idea to use the following checklist (prepared by the ethical committee of the European Therapy Studies Institute) to help you choose a professional for your teenager. An effective psychotherapist or counsellor:

- Knows how to build rapport quickly with distressed people
- Understands depression and how to lift it
- Helps immediately with anxiety problems, including trauma or fear-related symptoms
- Is prepared to give advice if needed or asked for
- Will not use jargon or tell you that counselling or psychotherapy has to be 'painful'
- Will not dwell unduly on the past
- Will be supportive when difficult feelings emerge, but will not encourage people to get emotional beyond the normal need to 'let go' of any bottled-up feelings
- May assist you in developing your social skills so that your needs for affection, friendship, pleasure, intimacy and connection to the wider community can be better fulfilled
- Will help you to draw and build on your own resources (which may prove greater than you thought)
- Will be considerate of the effects of counselling on the people close to you
- May teach you to relax deeply
- May help you think about your problems in new and more empowering ways
- Uses a wide range of techniques as appropriate
- May ask you to do things between sessions
- Will take as few sessions as possible
- Will increase your self-confidence and independence, and make sure you feel better after every consultation

Most importantly, an effective psychotherapist or counsellor can build rapport and relate to teenagers, can educate them about their brain and how it is developing, and come up with creative ways to help them overcome their problems without judgement and with compassion.

Talk to your GP or other health professional or check out the register of the Human Givens Institute for qualified Human Givens practitioners in your area.

Useful Resources

Barnardos
Barnardos works with families providing services and support throughout Ireland.
Barnardos, Christchurch Square, Dublin 8. Phone 01-453 0355, Callsave 1850 222 300
www.barnardos.ie

Childline
Childline is part of the ISPCC (Irish Society for the Prevention of Cruelty to Children) and has a telephone service, an online service and a texting service. Its aim is to empower, support and protect young people and its service is free and confidential.
Freephone 1800 666 666 or text 'Talk' to 50101
www.childline.ie

One Family
One Family aims to ensure a positive and equal future for all members of one-parent families in Ireland – changing attitudes, services, policies and lives.
One Family, Cherish House, 2 Lower Pembroke Street, Dublin 2.
Lo-Call 1890 662 212 or 01-6629212
www.onefamily.ie

Parentline
Parentline offers support, guidance and information on all aspects of being a parent.
Lo-Call 1890 927 277
www.parentline.ie

TeenLine Ireland
TeenLine is a free confidential phone and text service of emotional support dedicated to teenagers.
Freephone 1800 833 634 or text 'Teen' to 50015
www.teenline.ie

Tusla – Child and Family Agency
Tusla, the Child and Family Agency, is the dedicated State agency responsible for improving well-being and outcomes for children.
Floors 2–5, Brunel Building, Heuston South Quarter, Dublin 8. Phone 01-7718500
www.tusla.ie

Samaritans
The Samaritans offer a confidential emotional support service to individuals. This is provided through phone, email, text, postal or in person. Phone 116 123 or visit www.samaritans.org for details of your local branch and other contact details.

Youthreach
Youthreach is a Department of Education and Skills official education, training and work experience programme for early school-leavers. Please see your local branch online for telephone contact details.
www.youthreach.ie

Useful Websites

The Office for Internet Safety
The Office for Internet Safety was established by the Irish government to take a lead in responsibility for internet safety in Ireland, particularly as it relates to children. The Office for Internet Safety aims to build linkages and cohesion between all departments and agencies to ensure that the State provides the best possible protection for the community and promotes internet safety, particularly in relation to combating child pornography.
www.internetsafety.ie

Webwise
Webwise is the Irish Internet Safety Awareness Centre, which is co-funded by the Department of Education and Skills and the EU Safer Internet Programme. It is a useful resource for parents and teachers.
www.webwise.ie

Watch Your Space
Watch Your Space is an awareness-raising initiative, targeting teenagers, from Webwise. It is devoted to promoting safe, effective use of the internet among young people through awareness-raising resources and campaigns.
www.watchyourspace.ie

SpunOut.ie
SpunOut.ie is Ireland's youth information website created by young people, for young people. It aims to educate and inform readers about the importance of holistic well-being and how good health can be mantained, both physically and mentally.
www.spunout.ie

Useful Resources

Bully 4U
Bully 4u is a national not-for-profit organisation that provides anti-bullying services for primary and secondary schools in Ireland.
www.bully4u.ie

BullyingUK
This website is part of the Family Lives site and provides information on bullying.
www.bullying.co.uk

THE HUMAN GIVENS APPROACH

Information on the Human Givens approach and where to access a therapist in your area can be found at:
www.hgi.org.uk

Information on where to access a Human Givens therapist in your area can be found at:
www.hgi.org.uk/find-therapist

Information on training in the Human Givens Diploma course:
www.humangivenscollege.com and www.hgonlinecourses.com

Information on helping lift depression, the Human Givens approach:
www.lift-depression.com

Information on the Dublin Human Givens Centre:
www.dublinhumangivens.ie

ADDITIONAL READING

Biddulph, Steve (2013), *Steve Biddulph's Raising Girls*. London: Harper Thorsons.
Biegel, Gina M. (2009), *The Stress Reduction Workbook for Teens: Mindfulness Skills to Help You Deal with Stress*. Oakland, CA: Instant Help.
Brizendine, Louann (2007), *The Female Brain*. London: Bantam.
Brizendine, Louann (2011), *The Male Brain*. London: Bantam.
Bronson, Po and Merryman, Ashley (2011), *Nurtureshock: Why Everything We Thought about Children Is Wrong*. London: Ebury.
Brown, Grahame and Winn, Denise (2009), *How to Liberate Yourself from Pain: Practical Help for Sufferers*. Chalvington: HG Publishing.
Brown, Peter C. (2014), *Make It Stick: The Science of Successful Learning*. Cambridge, MA: Harvard University Press.
Cain, Susan (2013), *Quiet: The Power of Introverts in a World that Can't Stop Talking*. London: Viking.

Carey, Benedict (2014), *How We Learn: The Surprising Truth about When, Where, and Why It Happens*. London: Macmillan.

Cooke, Kaz (2009), *The Rough Guide to Girl Stuff*. London: Rough Guides.

Covey, Sean (2004), *7 Habits of Highly Effective Teenagers*. London: Simon & Schuster.

Dweck, Carol S. (2012), *Mindset: How You Can Fulfill Your Potential*. London: Robinson.

Faber, Adele, Mazlish, Elaine and Coe, Kimberly Ann (2006), *How to Talk so Teens Will Listen and Listen so Teens Will Talk*. London: Piccadilly.

Gilbert, Paul, (2010), *The Compassionate Mind: A New Approach to Life's Challenges*. London: Constable.

Griffin, Joe and Tyrrell, Ivan (2004), *Freedom from Addiction: The Secret behind Successful Addiction Busting*. Chalvington: Human Givens Publishing.

Griffin, Joe and Tyrrell, Ivan (2004), *How to Lift Depression: A Practical Handbook*. Chalvington: Human Givens Publishing.

Griffin, Joe and Tyrrell, Ivan (2004), *Human Givens: A New Approach to Emotional Health and Clear Thinking*. Chalvington: Human Givens Publishing.

Griffin, Joe and Tyrrell, Ivan (2008), *Release from Anger: Practical Help for Controlling Unreasonable Rage*. Chalvington: Human Givens Publishing.

Griffin, Joe and Tyrrell, Ivan (2014), *Why We Dream – The Definitive Answer: How Dreaming Keeps Us Sane, or Can Drive Us Mad*. Chalvington: Human Givens Publishing.

Griffin, Joe, Tyrrell, Ivan and Winn, Denise (2007), *How to Master Anxiety: A Practical Handbook*. Chalvington: Human Givens Publishing.

Harris, Judith Rich (1999), *The Nurture Assumption: Why Children Turn Out the Way They Do*. London: Bloomsbury.

Hines, Gill and Baverstock, Alison (2006), *Whatever! A Down-to-Earth Guide to Parenting Teenagers*. London: Piatkus.

Morgan, Nicola (2007), *Blame My Brain: The Amazing Teenage Brain Revealed*. London: Walker.

O'Hanlon, Brenda (1998), *Sleep: The Common Sense Approach*. Dublin: Gill & Macmillan.

O'Hanlon, Brenda (1998), *Stress: The Common Sense Approach*. Dublin: Gill & Macmillan.

Parsons, Rob (2009), *Teenagers! Helping Your Teenager Make It Through*. London: Hodder & Stoughton.

Peters, Steve (2011), *The Chimp Paradox: How Our Impulses and Emotions Can Determine Success and Happiness and How We Can Control Them*. London: Vermilion.

Riera, Michael (2012), *Uncommon Sense for Parents with Teenagers*. Berkeley, CA: Ten Speed.

Seligman, Martin E.P., Reivich, Karen, Jaycox, Lisa and Gillham, Jane (2007), *The Optimistic Child: A Proven Program to Safeguard Children against Depression and Build Lifelong Resilience*. Boston, MA: Houghton Mifflin.

Siegel, Daniel J. (2014), *Brainstorm: The Power and Purpose of the Teenage Brain*. New York, NY: Penguin.

Wiseman, Richard (2014), *Night School: Wake Up to the Power of Sleep*. London, Macmillian.

Wolf, Anthony E. and Franks, Suzanne (2002), *Get Out of My Life – But First Take Me and Alex into Town*. London, Profile.

Index

Index

Index